LET'S GET THING[S MOVING]

Pauline Chiarelli is a physiotherapist and specialist continence adviser who lives in Australia with her husband and children. Early professional experience in the field of pre-natal education led to Pauline developing an interest in training/retraining the muscles of the pelvic floor and she is now an expert in the treatment of urinary incontinence. Pauline has studied in the United Kingdom as well as Australia, has appeared in a number of international forums on continence, and is a sought-after media speaker. Her first book, *Women's Waterworks*, is an international bestseller.

Sue Markwell graduated with a Bachelor of Physiotherapy from the University of Queensland, Australia, in 1972. Valuable experience in women's health gained in Melbourne and Brisbane led to her joining the Lilian Cooper Medical Centre for Women to practice in pelvic floor dysfunction in 1988. Since 1989, she has also worked with surgeons at the Royal Brisbane Hospital in developing treatment programmes for disorders of defaecation. She lives with her husband and three children in Brisbane, Australia.

LET'S GET THINGS MOVING
Overcoming Constipation

PAULINE CHIARELLI and
SUE MARKWELL

ROBINSON
London

Robinson Publishing Ltd
7 Kensington Church Court
London W8 4SP

First published in Great Britain by
Robinson Publishing Ltd 1995

Published in Australia by
Gore & Osment Publications Pty Ltd

Copyright © Pauline Chiarelli and Sue Markwell 1992
Copyright © Gore & Osment Publications Pty Ltd

ISBN 1–85487–389–X

All rights reserved. This book is sold subject to the condition that it shall not, by way of trade or otherwise, be lent, re-sold, hired out or otherwise circulated in any form of binding or cover other than that in which it is published and without a similar condition including this condition being imposed on the subsequent purchaser.

A copy of the British Library Cataloguing in Publication Data is available from the British Library

Important Note
While this book has been written to explain normal bowel function and constipation and offers some advice on this troublesome complaint, it is in no way intended to take the place of a full examination by your own doctor. Seek medical advice if experiencing any persistent or unusual symptoms. While all care is taken, no responsibility can be accepted by the publisher, authors, editor or any person involved in the preparation of this book for loss occasioned to any person acting or refraining from action as a result of material in this book. Consult your doctor before commencing any health treatment.

Printed and bound in Great Britain

Contents

Introduction

1 **What Is Constipation?**   1
How common is constipation? – What is normal? – Other symptoms that can be associated with this problem.

2 **Inside Information**   7
Keeping things moving – What we've got and how it works – Using your bowels (defaecation).

3 **The Mysteries of Constipation**   22
Travel – Time – Changes in routine – Place – Food for thought – Pain – The menstrual cycle – Pregnancy – The new mother – Calling in the specialists – Wind and piles.

4 **Constipation in Young and Old**   35
Acute and chronic constipation in children – Causes of constipation in the elderly – Poor diet – Faecal impaction.

vi CONTENTS

5 Self-Help Strategies — 42
Fibre: facts and fallacies – How to increase your fibre and fluid intake – Massage – Activity – Sitting pretty – Laxatives.

6 Slow Transit Constipation — 55
Symptoms – Treatment.

7 Obstructed Defaecation — 60
Causes – Types – Diagnosis – Incontinence – Bladder and bowel problems.

8 The Pelvic Floor Muscles — 68
Feel it working – Find its limits – Force it higher – Helping the pelvic floor muscles – Functioning better.

9 Good Defaecation Dynamics — 80
Putting it all together – Learning how to 'pump-brace' – How to empty a megarectum.

10 Tests – Searching for Clues — 88
X-ray tests – Endoscopy – Functional tests.

11 Surgery — 93
'Rubber banding' – Sphincterotomy – Rectopexy – Proctectomy – Colectomy – Colostomy – Ileostomy.

Glossary — 97
Explaining the terms.

Introduction

Whether we like to admit it or not, we have all been brought up to regard the regularity of our bowels as an important part of our personal health routine. In the Western world, we are made aware of our bowel habits at a very early age. Mothers begin potty training babies from as early as six months of age. The resulting delivery of the 'prize' is made a great fuss of by the mother, but children are taught that it is considered to be dirty, smelly and disgusting . . . a very confusing state of affairs for children in their early years, especially at a time when they are trying to understand the idea of cause and effect, and most of all, trying to please Mother.

Many of you will recall the emphasis placed on the daily motion during childhood, and the weekly dose of 'moving medicine' – usually castor oil or paraffin – administered on a Saturday whether you needed it or not, to keep you regular. The drive for 'inner cleanliness' went on and on. Is it any wonder many of us believe that as the sun revolves around the earth, so our bowels should operate with clockwork regularity every single day?

Constipation. A taboo subject; suffered in silence, rarely discussed by genteel folks. And yet it is a condition that has been experienced by each and every one of us at some point in our lives. The economic costs of constipation are staggering. In the United States alone, $330 million a year is spent on over-the-counter laxatives!

This book has been written to help you understand something about your 'inner secrets'. It will unravel the mysteries of those deep and hidden recesses within your body – your bowels – and how food gets from one end to the other.

It provides information about the alimentary canal or gastrointestinal tract (the medical terms for the bowels) and the waste product – faeces, sometimes called a stool.

The book takes a comprehensive look at a condition that is shrouded in social sensitivities. In writing it, we hoped to answer your many questions and to provide useful information to help you towards better health and wellbeing. If it is at all helpful, then we have been successful.

Pauline Chiarelli and Sue Markwell

Chapter 1
What is Constipation?

Constipation is not a disease but a symptom, and can mean different things to different people. There are a number of conditions that can cause constipation. However, there are still three basic descriptions commonly given by people suffering from this uncomfortable condition. They complain about:

- The stools themselves – too hard, too large, too small.
- Passing the stool – they have to strain and push.
- The frequency of the stool – they don't feel the need to go as often as they think they should.

Each of these complaints tells a slightly different story. They tell us that constipation might be a problem concerning five things:

THE COMMANDER (the brain)
THE CONTENTS (the stool or faeces)
THE CONDUIT (the bowel)

THE CONTAINER	(the anorectum – where the anus and rectum come together)
THE CONTROL	(the muscle function)

One definition of constipation might be the infrequent passage of stools – less than three times per week. However, if you have to push and strain excessively to empty your bowel, if you feel the need to go each day but simply 'can't get it out', or if you go each day only to pass rock-hard little pellets, then you could consider yourself constipated.

HOW COMMON IS CONSTIPATION?

Constipation is man's most common chronic digestive condition, with one person in six (15 per cent) complaining of it. Surveys show that about 6 per cent of children are reported to be constipated, with boys the main victims. This trend is reversed in adulthood, and women are far more likely to suffer from this problem than men. However, these differences even out as we grow older, and constipation is common in the elderly of both sexes.

Constipation increases with age, becoming much more frequent and much more serious. Almost half of those admitted into acute geriatric wards are suffering from severe constipation, as are 80 per cent of elderly people living in residential care.

WHAT IS NORMAL?

- **Regularity:** Normal frequency of bowel motions lies somewhere between three times a day and three times a week. For most people, defaecation occurs once a day, in the morning. The call of nature is felt and answered effortlessly, painlessly and with a great sense of a 'job well done' when it is all over.
- **Colour:** The colour of your stool is brown because the bacteria living in the bowel make brown pigment out of bile acids and salts. These acids and salts are present in the bile, a digestive fluid manufactured by the liver, which is used as part of the digestion process in the small intestine.

The stool colour might vary slightly from day to day and is often related to the food that you have eaten (but can also signal problems, so should not be ignored). For example, liquorice or iron tablets can turn your stool black; but if it turns black without your taking either, it suggests bleeding somewhere in the intestine and you should seek medical advice without delay. Your stool might become red if you eat beetroot, but bright red blood in the toilet or on the toilet paper should send you off to the doctor immediately. Bleeding piles (haemorrhoids) are the most likely cause of obvious bleeding, but a thorough examination is required to

make sure that the bleeding is not from some other area inside your bowel.
- **Odour:** Your stool smells as it does because of chemicals produced by bacteria within the bowel. They work on the undigested fibres and sugars in the stool to form gas.
- **Consistency:** As the faeces move along through the bowel, they normally become drier. This drying process is a delicate balance – the stool should be well formed enough to be squeezed/pushed along the large bowel, but moist enough to pass along painlessly.

The longer the stool takes to move through the system, the drier and harder it becomes, eventually turning to hard-to-pass pellets.

NOT ONLY, BUT ALSO

People who suffer from constipation often complain of other symptoms as well. These include:

- Headache.
- Tiredness and lack of energy.
- Bad breath.
- Difficulty in concentrating.
- Loss of appetite.
- Coating on the tongue.
- Bloating of the abdomen.
- Wind.
- Skin problems.

Chapter 2
Inside Information

The human body is a miraculous maze of interconnected systems that all work together in harmony as you go about the business of living. Each of these systems needs different fuel (nutrients) to keep it going – nutrients obtained from eating a wide variety of foods. We put this food in one end and faeces emerge from the other end some days later. The alimentary canal has delicate, highly specialised mechanisms along its whole length, designed to extract the nourishment necessary for every cell in the human body. Some areas have glands which add substances to the food, while others have a lining adapted to removing substances from the food.

KEEPING THINGS MOVING

Gut motility is the term used to describe the muscular activity necessary to move the food through the alimentary canal. This is a combined squeeze and push movement, just like

8 LET'S GET THINGS MOVING

the one you use when you are trying to squeeze a frozen iceblock out of its plastic tray. To do this, it is necessary to have muscle that is capable of squeezing, nerves that are capable of relaying the messages to squeeze, and a brain that controls both the muscles and the nerves. There are special reflexes involved.

Motility is affected by:

- The amount of food or faeces in any part of the system.
- Their chemical make-up.
- The effects of gut hormones (there are over 300 types!).
- 'Stop/go' switches working within the nerve network.
- Female sex hormones.
- Your emotions.

WHAT WE'VE GOT AND HOW IT WORKS

Many parts of the body go to make up the alimentary tract:

- **The Mouth:** The complex process of digestion and elimination begins with the mouth. As we chew food, it becomes coated with saliva and a reflex action tells the glands inside the stomach to 'get ready, food is on its way'. These glands start to secrete acids and other substances which will help digest the food about to be swallowed.

INSIDE INFORMATION 9

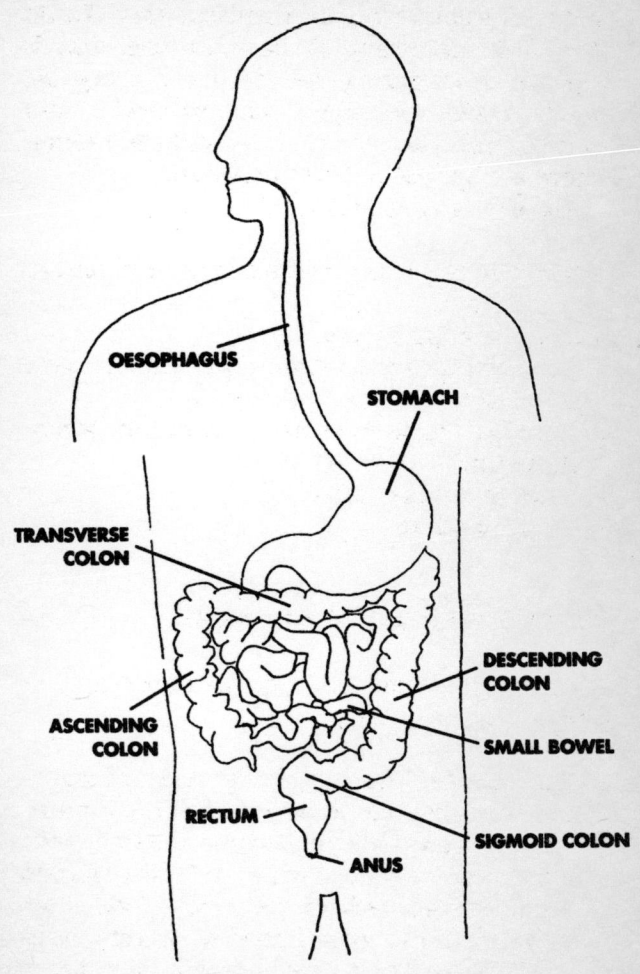

10 LET'S GET THINGS MOVING

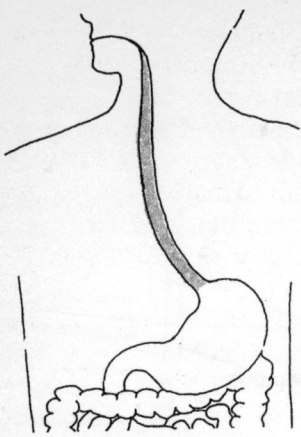

The Oesophagus

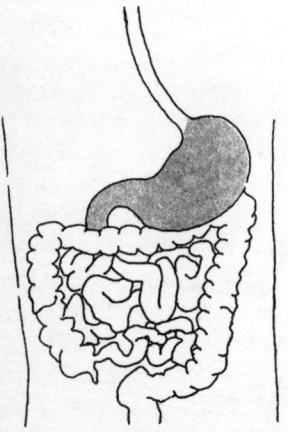

The Stomach

- **The Oesophagus:** The food pipe from the mouth to the stomach is called the oesophagus. This clever tube has to cope with food as different in size and texture as peanuts and ice-cream, or banana and Coca-Cola, as well as gulps of air that are taken in along with the food. It carries the food down into the stomach, and stops it from coming up again.

- **The Stomach:** The stomach is a hollow muscular churn, a bit like a food processor, which prepares food for digestion. It has two jobs: it chops up the food as the first part of the digestive process (at this stage the food is called **chyme**); and it holds the processed food until the small intestine or bowel (where the absorption of nutrients takes place) is ready for it. The stomach lining is very special: tough enough to withstand damage from rough or sharp-edged foodstuffs, as well as being able to cope with its own acids and digestive juices. When really stretched, the stomach can hold up to a litre of food and fluid, but we generally experience a sense of fullness when half a litre is present.

  Motility (movement) between the stomach itself and the small intestine depends on reflexes, which make sure that food is moved through the system just as it should be. It is pushed along by the muscles within the walls of the whole alimentary canal in a wave of movement called **peristalsis**. These

12 LET'S GET THINGS MOVING

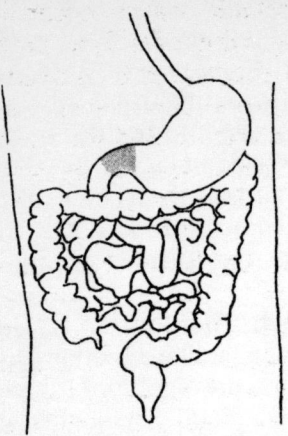

The Pyloric Sphincter

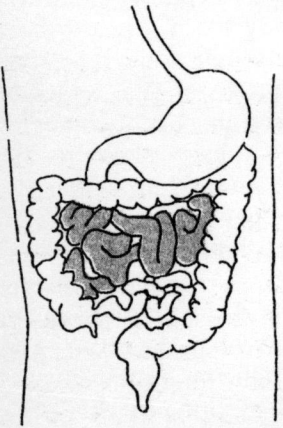

The Small Intestine or Small Bowel

strong peristaltic waves occur four to six times a day, whenever food enters the stomach, and the waves of movement propel the bowel contents onwards ... ultimately towards the rectum and the anus. An average mixed meal leaves the stomach after about two to four hours.

- **The Pyloric Sphincter:** The outlet valve of the stomach is called the pyloric sphincter. Just how this valve knows when to open and release a little chyme into the small intestine is not well understood. Once food passes through this valve, it will not normally move backwards again, even if you stand on your head! Everything in a normal, healthy gastrointestinal tract moves in the one direction.

- **The Small Intestine or Small Bowel:** The small intestine is a continuous tube, three to six cm in diameter and up to five metres long. Its first section is called the **duodenum**, and this is where most of the digestion process takes place. The liver, the gall bladder and the pancreas all secrete special chemicals called enzymes into the food mixture in the duodenum. It is the job of these enzymes to change the complicated fats, proteins and carbohydrates in food into simpler chemical structures that can be absorbed through the wall of the intestine into the bloodstream. The special lining of the small intestine is covered by tiny hair-like fingers which allow nutrients to pass through from the intestine into the bloodstream, thence to be transported to all parts of the body that need them.

- After the duodenum comes the **jejunum** and then the **ileum**. These sections of the small intestine form many loops which can move freely among one another as the chyme passes from one segment to another. After leaving the stomach, an average-sized meal takes about four hours to pass through the small intestine before it gets to the large bowel (colon). This movement of food along the small intestine is called gastric motility.

  Whenever fresh food enters the stomach, a valve between the small bowel and the colon opens, moving the remains from earlier meals into the large bowel.

- **The Large Intestine or Large Bowel (colon):** About two litres of chyme empties from the small intestine into the colon each day. The colon begins at the **caecum** where another valve (the **ileocaecal valve**) stops the bowel contents from moving backwards. They travel from the lower right-hand corner of the abdomen, up to under the right rib cage (the **ascending colon**), across the top of the abdominal cavity (the **transverse colon**), and down the left side (the **descending colon**), following the shape of the letter n.

INSIDE INFORMATION 15

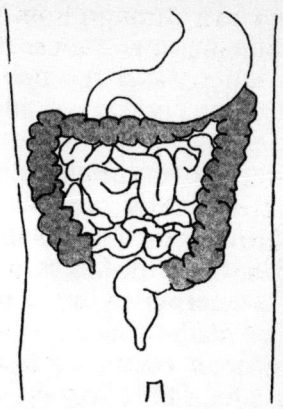

The Large Intestine or Large Bowel

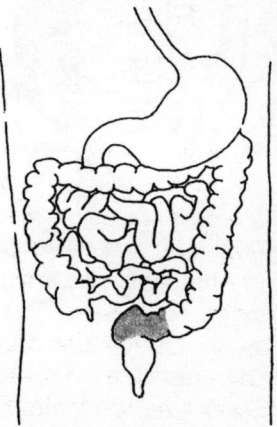

The Sigmoid Colon

16 LET'S GET THINGS MOVING

- They now enter the last loop of the colon – the **sigmoid colon**, which leads down to the **rectum** and then the **anal canal**. The sigmoid colon may act as a brake, keeping faeces back from the rectum. Food residue takes one to three days to move through the gut. Ninety per cent of this time is spent moving through the colon. This is called the colon transit time. The speed at which the faeces moves through the colon is determined by the food we have eaten. It is made longer by eating meals containing a lot of fat, and shortened by food with a high fibre content.

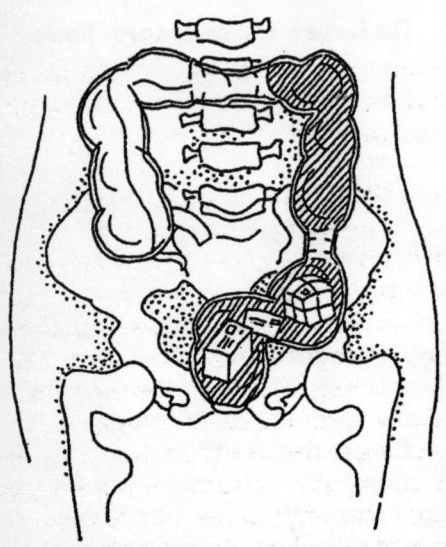

Packaging and despatch

INSIDE INFORMATION 17

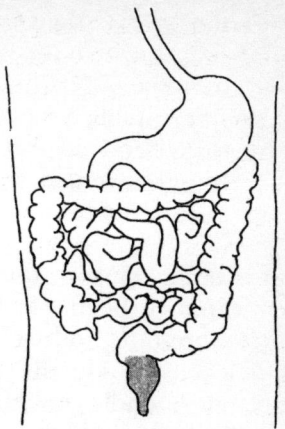

The Rectum

Faeces dry out during their journey along the colon; they are dried out, packaged ready for despatch via the rectum.

- **The Rectum:** The presence of the stool in the descending colon starts up a wave of peristalsis, which now moves the faecal mass downward and into the rectum. This is the last part of the gastro-intestinal tract. It is a special muscular tube, through which the faeces move just before being passed out through the anus. It is about 30cm (12 inches) long.

  As long as the stool remains in the descending colon, the rectum remains empty and there is no urge to use the bowels. The presence of a stool within the rectum sends out a signal that the bowels need to be emptied.

LET'S GET THINGS MOVING

This process ideally occurs one or more times a day, but its timing depends on many factors – arising outside the body as well as inside. The urge to go can be put off again and again, but most people establish a regular pattern and the urge to go is felt either in the morning soon after getting out of bed, in the evening, or following food or drink.

- **The Anal Canal:** This is the end of the alimentary canal. It begins at the **anorectal junction**, is three to four centimetres in length and leads outside the body. It contains many nerve endings which are highly sensitive to pain, and which help determine whether the rectal contents are solid, liquid or gas. It has a well-developed blood supply, the veins of which cause one of the most common medical complaints in existence – **haemorrhoids**, also known as piles.

- **The Anal Canal and the Pelvic Floor Muscles:** We can choose to put off emptying the bowel until the time and the place is suitable. The group of muscles that provide this control surrounds the anus or the outlet and is called the anal sphincter. This is a very complicated group of muscles which are categorised medically as either **deep** or **superficial sphincters**. They work together with the muscles of the pelvic floor (more about these important muscles in Chapter 8). The pelvic floor muscles that work with the anal sphincter are called the **levators**, which means 'the lifters'. Simply put, the levators support the contents of the pelvis, while the sphincters open and close the anus. There is an important relationship between all these muscles and the angle at which the rectum joins to the anus. If the pelvic floor muscles are strong and have good tone, they help the deep and superficial sphincters to provide a pressure zone, which in part works like a valve.

- The superficial sphincters are categorised into **internal** and **external anal sphincters**. Most of the anal pressure is provided by the internal sphincter, which is extremely important in helping us not to lose control of our bowels. This is not under our conscious control. The external anal muscle works voluntarily to help us 'hold on'. All these muscles work to maintain a closed anus, even during sleep. But to do this they need to be in peak condition. Damage to any one of these structures can threaten our ability to control our bowels.

USING YOUR BOWELS (DEFAECATION)

This is something most of us do every day with quite a sense of accomplishment. It is also something that we take entirely for granted. Let's look at the normal sequence of events. When the stool in the sigmoid colon becomes large enough, reflex contractions (peristalsis)

20 LET'S GET THINGS MOVING

begin to move the stool down into the rectum. We feel the need to go, or as we often say, 'Nature calls'. Special nerves within the muscles of the pelvic floor help us to feel that the stool is ready to be expelled (if these special nerves are damaged, then the 'time to go' sensation is only felt when the stool is extremely large). The rectum stretches to hold the stool while the internal anal sphincter relaxes and the external sphincter contracts. This allows for 'sampling'. About 30ml of whatever is present in the bowel moves across highly sensitive nerve endings. These special nerve endings allow us to determine if these contents are solid (a stool), liquid (diarrhoea), or gas (wind). This sampling process is done subconsciously.

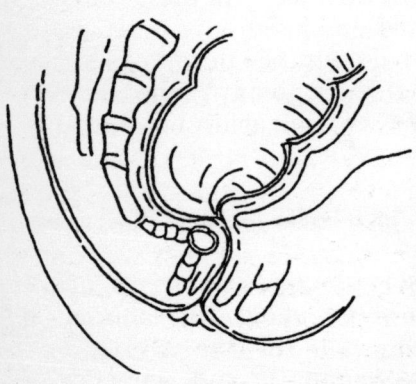

At rest, sphincter muscles are closed

INSIDE INFORMATION 21

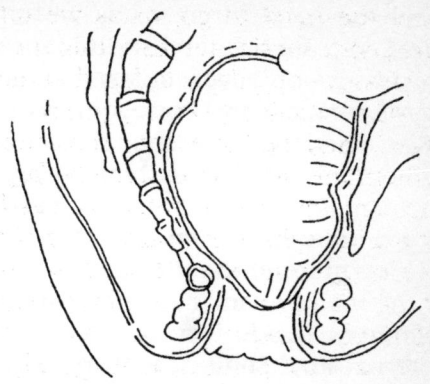

When muscles open out, a funnel is made and emptying occurs

When the contents reach about 150–200ml, we then make the conscious decision to respond. Sometimes problems can arise, interfering with the proper functioning of the sampling process, but normally we can hold in the solids and let the gases escape to allow more room in the rectum while waiting to use the toilet. If we get the message that the stool in the rectum is liquid (diarrhoea), then the external anal sphincter squeezes the anus shut and we make haste to get to the toilet. These muscles need to be in perfect working order to be able to provide good control in these situations.

If the decision is made to empty the bowel because the stool is solid and the toilet is nearby, we take up the sitting position and begin to push. From childhood, most people are able to use their abdominal and anal muscles together to create a funnel so that faeces pass through easily. However, it is worth mentioning that if we want our bowels to work under the best conditions, we should take up the **squatting position**, rather than simply sitting on the toilet. Squatting allows the anal canal to be opened more fully from front to back, making a much more efficient funnel.

Pushing causes an increase in pressure within the abdomen. This in turn causes the external and internal anal sphincters to relax and the pelvic floor drops down to form a funnel. The outlet of this funnel is the top of the anal canal. Repeating the pressure (pushing, grunting) moves the stool downward and empties the bowel. Sometimes the whole of the descending colon can be cleared at one time, but usually only the rectum is emptied.

A lot of effort is needed to pass small pellet-like stools because they are not bulky enough to relax the anal sphincter muscles properly. People with irritable bowel syndrome who complain of constipation will be only too familiar with this problem. Soft faeces in a container that doesn't squeeze properly can be just as difficult to expel as pellets.

When emptying is complete, a closing reflex takes over – the internal anal sphincter closes and the pelvic floor muscles resume their supporting role. These muscles must be strong and healthy if they are to support the sphincters in the proper position to contract and relax as required.

Sometimes, however, these muscles aren't strong and don't support the sphincters. Some of us don't use them properly. We may have developed bad habits, and may need to relearn how to defaecate efficiently (for more on this, see Chapters 8 and 9).

Chapter 3
The Mysteries of Constipation

You are said to be constipated when passing your stool becomes less frequent or more difficult than usual. Using laxatives is not the solution to constipation resulting from infection or dietary change, though many usually sensible people think exactly the opposite and insist on taking them.

Some older people believe that poisonous toxins are absorbed into the body if they do not use their bowels regularly. So they may take daily doses of fruit salts or liver salts in the belief that it is essential to clean out the bowels at least once a week. This simple biological function can become the focus of all their energy and attention. Any slight difference to the usual pattern is seen as abnormal, leading to worry, anxiety and, in turn, more irregularity.

However, your bowels work in a regular rhythm. They are only one part of an incredibly sensitive group of systems, all synchronised around you – your personal needs and personality. A change in rhythm is usually noticeable to us. Sometimes its cause is obvious, and it may be put right by simply looking at your lifestyle, recognising any changes and making a few adjustments. It may require a bit of detective work, but by looking at the following, you may be able to solve the mystery of your constipation yourself!

TRAVEL

This is probably the easiest cause to recognise. International travel and jet lag can cause an amazing change in bowel habits. When we travel, we often cross into different time zones, and it can take weeks to get back into the swing of things. It is very strange to find yourself getting out of bed at 2 a.m. to use your bowels! It can also be difficult to cope with tiny aeroplane toilets, particularly with other passengers queueing outside. When we go on holiday we eat different foods at different times, and drink water with a different mineral content from that at home. All this can play havoc with our normal bowel rhythm. You can probably recall the pleasure of returning home – the sense of relief and comfort you feel when you sit on your very own toilet. At last it is possible to relax – and relaxation is one of the most important tools we use to trigger all those complicated reflexes necessary to empty our bowels.

TIME

The demands of a hectic lifestyle grow and grow, until we seem to be constantly rushing everywhere to meet some new deadline or crisis! We simply don't have enough time, which can have two effects on bowel rhythm:
1. It causes us to become stressed and anxious and leads to tension in some of the muscle groups of the body, as well as changes in bowel motility.
2. It causes us to rush through a bowel motion instead of taking our time about it. In extreme cases, the urge to empty the bowels is ignored time and time again.

CHANGES IN ROUTINE

Has your daily routine changed? This can involve changes to all manner of things, from your sleeping habits to your job description, and all these changes can affect your bowels.

- Has your sleeping pattern altered so that the time you get up has changed?
- Do you drive the children to school now instead of walking them there and back?
- Have your work hours been altered? If opening your bowels is something you do early in your day, even half an hour can make a difference.

THE MYSTERIES OF CONSTIPATION 27

- Have you changed your method of travelling to work or the route you take to get there? These can all change the time you need to get up out of bed.
- At work, have your regular duties been altered in any way?
- Has your exercise regime changed?

PLACE

- Has your work place altered, making the toilet less accessible?
- Is the toilet itself suitable to use? Is it a different toilet?
- Do you have to ask permission to go to the toilet? Is this an embarrassing situation for you?
- Do you feel in any way inhibited when you use the toilet at work?
- Are you busier at work, unable to answer the call to go?
- A trip to hospital can really put your bowel pattern out of whack! Apart from fasting for surgery, your daily activities are far from normal. Lying in bed for just 24 hours robs the body of a whole range of movement and activity, as well as making it impossible for gravity to help things keep moving – so imagine the effect of being confined to bed for seven days! To say nothing of the effects of surgery itself, or the indignities of using a bedpan surrounded by a ward full of other

people. Balancing on a cold, hard bedpan <u>never</u> helps anyone to relax properly and concentrate on the job at hand.

FOOD FOR THOUGHT

Most of us have an eating pattern that we automatically follow (though we don't necessarily eat what is best for us – see Chapter 5 for more on food). It has often been said that we are what we eat, and that any change in your eating pattern must soon be reflected in your bowel motions.

Questions that you might ask yourself about your eating pattern include:

- Have you started a weight reduction programme?
- Have you been fasting – perhaps for religious reasons, or to prepare for some medical test?
- Are you on some sort of fad diet? Eating only bananas or apples for three days would change all sorts of rhythms, not only in the bowel!
- Has your daily routine – <u>when</u> as well as <u>what</u> you eat – changed in any way?
- Are you drinking your normal amount of fluid?
- Have you changed the <u>nature</u> of your fluid intake? For example, you might drink coffee now because there is no refrigerator at work to keep your orange juice cool, or perhaps

you've switched to cans of cola because you no longer have access to tea-making facilities.
- Are you taking any drugs that might be affecting your bowel pattern? Do not hesitate to speak to your doctor about this.

PAIN

The perineum is that part of the body between the legs, bounded at the back by the tip of the tailbone and in front by the pubic bone. Any pain in this area makes defaecating an unpleasant experience, as bearing down tends to increase any perineal discomfort. Abdominal pain – due to having your period, perhaps, or caused by such things as endometriosis or adhesions – might also make bearing down difficult. Haemorrhoids, fissures or small tears in the skin of the anal canal can cause pain during a bowel motion, as can any skin irritation around the front or back passage. (**NB: Any pain or discomfort in these areas should always be reported to your doctor.**) Of the many reflexes involved in emptying your bowels, one of the most important 'on-switches' is relaxation of the pelvic floor – not easy if you have a sore bottom or pain in the abdomen. Once this relaxation reflex is disrupted, even when the source of pain has gone, it can sometimes be difficult to get all the muscles relaxed easily. This is especially so with children, whose constipation often begins with a tiny fissure or crack in the wall of the anus.

THE MENSTRUAL CYCLE

One in six women has a problem with constipation in the last half of the menstrual cycle, due to the action of female hormones.

PREGNANCY

Constipation is quite common during pregnancy. During this time, the influence of hormones can lead to a slower transit time for the movement of food through the body as some of the smooth muscles of the colon become sluggish.

THE NEW MOTHER

It is often at this stage that future problems develop. Post-natal constipation is due to many factors:

- The fluid levels within the body go through amazing changes as the breasts begin to produce milk for the new baby.
- The perineum is tender, even painful, following delivery, whether there are stitches from a tear or episiotomy or not.
- The new mother's daily routine is thrown out with the bath water. She has no time for herself now; not even the luxury of the time

THE MYSTERIES OF CONSTIPATION 31

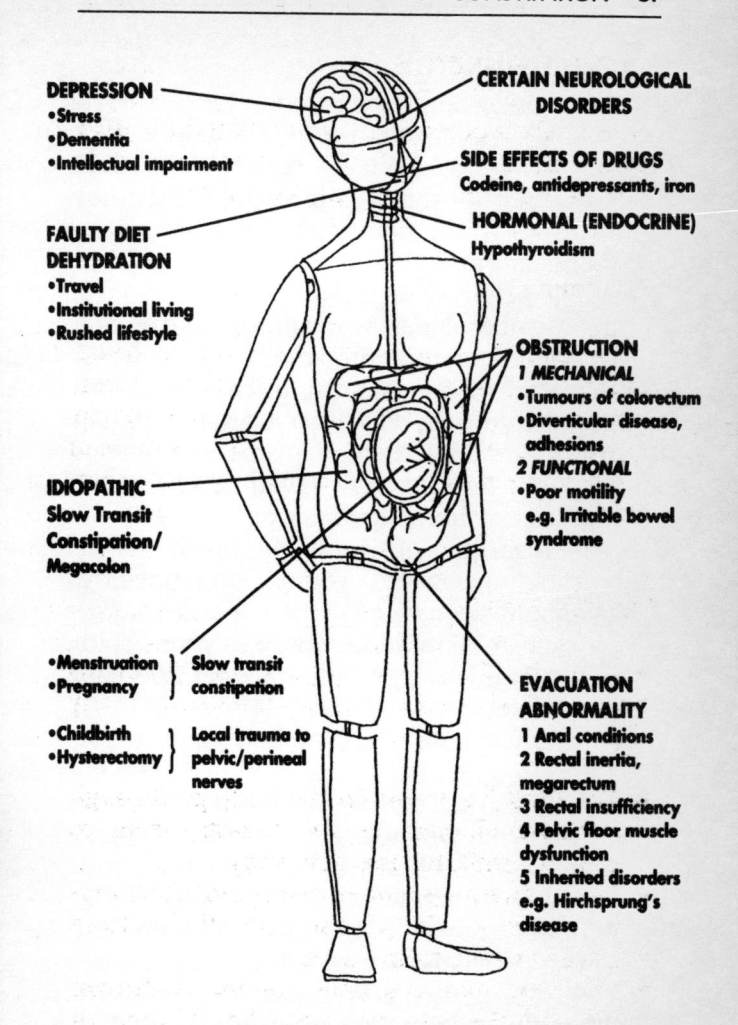

DEPRESSION
- Stress
- Dementia
- Intellectual impairment

CERTAIN NEUROLOGICAL DISORDERS

SIDE EFFECTS OF DRUGS
Codeine, antidepressants, iron

HORMONAL (ENDOCRINE)
Hypothyroidism

FAULTY DIET DEHYDRATION
- Travel
- Institutional living
- Rushed lifestyle

OBSTRUCTION
1 MECHANICAL
- Tumours of colorectum
- Diverticular disease, adhesions

2 FUNCTIONAL
- Poor motility e.g. Irritable bowel syndrome

IDIOPATHIC
Slow Transit Constipation/Megacolon

- Menstruation } Slow transit
- Pregnancy } constipation

- Childbirth } Local trauma to
- Hysterectomy } pelvic/perineal nerves

EVACUATION ABNORMALITY
1. Anal conditions
2. Rectal inertia, megarectum
3. Rectal insufficiency
4. Pelvic floor muscle dysfunction
5. Inherited disorders e.g. Hirchsprung's disease

CAUSES OF CONSTIPATION

normally taken for a relaxed bowel movement.
- The muscles and nerve supply of the pelvic floor are damaged during childbirth. It is unusual for women to regain more than 75 per cent of the muscle strength that they had prior to the delivery of their baby.
- Special attention must be paid to the muscles of the pelvic floor if you want to avoid a lifetime of problems with constipation as well as bladder control problems. This is when they start in the majority of cases, and this is where you can do a great job in preventing future problems. Follow all the instructions for pelvic floor exercise given in Chapter 8; begin them immediately after your baby is born, regardless of how many stitches or any bruising you have. If you are breastfeeding, this might slow your progress a little, but do not give up! If in doubt, speak to your health visitor about your programme and how you are progressing.
- The pelvic floor muscles and their nerve supply might take up to 12 months to recover from the delivery. It is a good idea to support your perineum every time you open your bowels because, just as they were damaged by stretching as you pushed the baby out, they can be damaged as you bear down while defaecating. So in the early postnatal stage, place your hand in front of the anus and gently press upwards as you bear down. This prevents the pelvic floor from

ballooning downwards, damaging the nerves to the muscles over and over. Two out of every 10 women strain and push to use their bowels!

CALLING IN THE SPECIALISTS

Not all of the mysteries of constipation have simple solutions. If the clues given so far do not seem to have brought you any closer to solving your particular mystery, read on. Your problem may be due to other conditions such as the following, which require specialist diagnosis and attention.

BEING A WOMAN

Pregnancy and childbirth are not the only problems to be considered. Others include:
- **Slow transit constipation** – in which everything moves through the system very slowly – is a condition some women experience. It begins in childhood for at least 50 per cent of women suffering it, and a further 20 per cent of cases will have trouble in their teenage years. More about this in Chapter 6.
- **Motility problems** can be directly related to female sex hormones. These hormones play an important role in the way that messages are transferred along the nerves within the gastro-intestinal tract.

- **Hysterectomy** (in which the uterus and sometimes the ovaries are removed) is one of the most commonly performed female operations. Many women complain that their bladder and bowel problems begin immediately following hysterectomy. Problems arise when damage occurs to those nerves that control many of the reflexes that give us good bladder and bowel function. In some cases, the problems are present before surgery but become more severe afterwards.

IRRITABLE BOWEL SYNDROME

This term refers to a condition in which the colon starts behaving erratically. It is sometimes called a spastic colon. Symptoms include changes in bowel habits such as constipation and diarrhoea, distension, pain and flatulence.

DIVERTICULAR DISEASE

Diverticular disease occurs when the wall of the colon becomes weak and small sacs form within the bowel wall. This process is called **diverticulosis**. When the sacs become inflamed, **diverticulitis** results and bowel function is altered, resulting in such problems as diarrhoea, constipation, pain and bloody stools.

TUMOURS

Benign and malignant tumours may develop in both the colon and the rectum. These tumours may obstruct the movement of faeces along the bowel, resulting in constipation.

AND WHILE WE'RE ON THE SUBJECT . . .

Since we've already broken the ice on one unmentionable subject, let's look at two other common problems that people often feel too embarrassed to talk about – **wind** and **piles** (haemorrhoids).

Passing wind (flatulence) is a normal daily occurrence for most people. But for some, it can be quite a problem – involving too much wind, bloating and abdominal pain.

Wind, or flatus, is made up of hydrogen, carbon dioxide, nitrogen and sometimes methane (this is the smelly ingredient). The total amount of wind passed in one day varies between 200 mls to 2,400 mls; 25–100 mls may be passed per episode. Less is passed through the night. Two-thirds of the flatus is formed by the bacteria which cause fermentation in the bowel, the rest being made up of air that is swallowed as you eat.

If you drink fizzy drinks, some of the gas will pass into the intestines and eventually make its way through the other end. Burping is almost

36 LET'S GET THINGS MOVING

entirely due to swallowed air. If you are bothered by wind, try to eat much more slowly to make sure that you are not swallowing air. Then you might consider giving up beer and carbonated soft drinks. Finally, you might have to try a diet that cuts out, in turn, milk, beans, cabbage and onions.

If you happen to be a 'methane producer', there isn't much you can do about it. It may be some consolation to know that while smelly wind is highly embarrassing, it is perhaps the least dangerous of all bowel problems. Flatulence can even have a positive aspect: for instance, after abdominal surgery it's a sign that the function of your intestines is improving.

Piles, or haemorrhoids, are varicose veins in the lining of the anorectum. They bleed very easily and first may be noticed with blood appearing in the toilet pan or on toilet paper. **(NB: Anyone who bleeds from the anus must be examined by a doctor.)** Even though piles are a very common cause of anal bleeding and even if you know you have a haemorrhoid, play it safe and get it checked out.

Haemorrhoids can cause discomfort or extreme pain; and may make going to the toilet difficult; and sometimes require surgery. By changing your diet so that you don't strain when using your bowels, you may keep this annoying problem under control. It's a good idea to wash – not wipe – your anus after a bowel movement. Pre-moistened towelettes are excellent for this.

Chapter 4
Constipation in Young and Old

Little people can have big problems, and constipation is quite common in children. It is twice as likely to affect boys as girls. It can occur after an illness or a bout of diarrhoea, after a holiday or change in diet, or when the child is excited or worried about something. It can also follow where the child is trying to avoid using the school toilets – perhaps because of bullying or teasing, because they are unclean or have no paper, or because they are badly lit and frightening.

- **Acute constipation:** When this is a short-term problem it is called acute constipation. You should always seek medical advice, but generally speaking, if the cause is known, then simply correcting the problem might be enough. However, acute constipation can easily become a long-term problem which is much more difficult to treat.
- **Chronic constipation:** Soiling is often the most noticeable sign when a child is suffering

from this condition – frequent soiling, involving small quantities of fluid or semi-solid faeces. This happens when there is a huge mass of stool in the rectum. This mass holds the anorectal angle open and stimulates the formation of mucus which escapes, causing soiling.

NB: **This condition should always be managed under medical supervision. It is important to begin the proper treatment for the individual problem and to sort it out before the child starts school.**

CONSTIPATION AND THE ELDERLY

'The only things that improve with age are compound interest and red wine.' Statements like these would have us believe that everything starts to fall apart as we move towards old age. While this is to some degree a myth, unhappily, in the case of constipation, it tends to be true. Thirty per cent of elderly people take laxatives and many believe that a weekly purge is necessary, whether their bowel motions are regular or not. They don't realise that laxatives are drugs and have very definite side effects.

As with children, the elderly can suffer from two types of constipation – acute and chronic – and these have many causes (see chart).

Acute constipation (with a fairly sudden onset) could be a warning sign of some underlying problem and should be checked out by your doctor.

CAUSES OF CONSTIPATION IN THE ELDERLY

Physical

- Haemorrhoids
- Painful tears around the anus
- Weak abdominal muscles
- Weak anal sphincters/pelvic floor muscles
- Reduced physical activities
- Less efficient digestion of food
- Less efficient absorption of nutrients into the bloodstream
- Ageing of nervous system, affecting muscle coordination
- Less efficient digestion of food
- Reduced kidney function
- Reduced reflex speed

Psychological

- Depression
- Loneliness
- Bereavement
- Emotional crises

Drugs

- Anti-Parkinson's medication
- Anti-depressants
- Sleeping tablets
- Tranquillisers
- Codeine

CAUSES OF POOR DIET IN THE ELDERLY

- Dental problems
- Ill-fitting dentures
- Less ability to get around
- Restricted access to shopping and food variety
- Chronic illness
- Poor eyesight
- Reduced production of saliva
- Loss of sense of taste
- Loss of sense of smell
- Poor memory
- Financial and social problems
- Lack of transport
- Confusion at supermarket
- Poor cooking facilities
- Food prices
- Stress
- Living alone
- Apathy
- Overuse of vitamins
- Overuse of unprocessed bran
- Loss of appetite caused by prescription drugs
- Poor eating habits

The most common form of constipation in the elderly, however, has a gradual onset; over months or even years, the bowels are emptied a little less frequently than previously until eventually a stool is passed only about once every four or five days.

Any person who is not physically active will notice a change in bowel frequency because, as we've seen, movement is a very important trigger for the gastro-colic reflex. This is why elderly people who are very inactive often become severely constipated, particularly those in long-term care.

A combination of factors can worsen the problem. For example, being confined to bed slows the colon transit time. Trying to use a bedpan doesn't help matters, nor does being unable to go to the toilet as soon as the call is felt, a change in eating or drinking patterns, or anxiety about having to be in bed in the first place. It all adds up to a real merry-go-round of minor problems, working together to cause a major constipation problem.

FAECAL IMPACTION

If unattended, severe constipation becomes faecal impaction. Symptoms of faecal impaction are diarrhoea and loss of control of the anal sphincter. If the rectum becomes packed full of faeces, the anorectal angle is held open and the sphincters do not operate properly. The mass of faeces irritates the lining of the rectum and mucus is produced. This mucus runs along the faecal mass and leaks out like diarrhoea. As with children, this process can result in frequent soiling – several times daily – with small amounts of fluid or semi-solid faeces.

42 LET'S GET THINGS MOVING

FAECAL IMPACTION

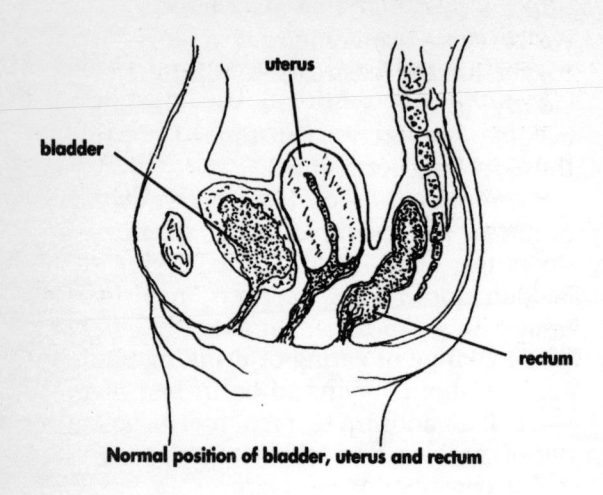

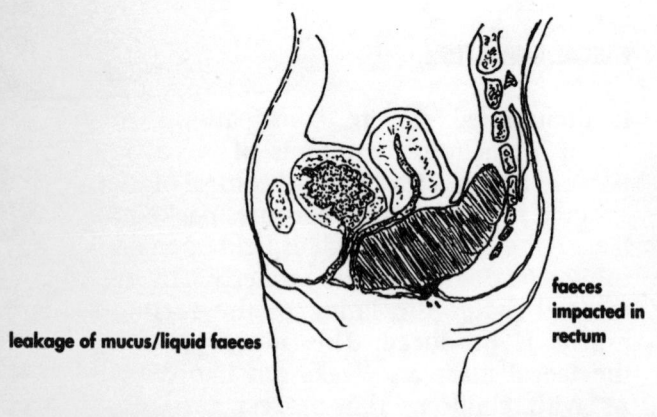

Normal position of bladder, uterus and rectum

(labels: uterus, bladder, rectum)

Full rectum pushes forward on bladder and can cause urinary symptoms

(labels: leakage of mucus/liquid faeces, faeces impacted in rectum)

- **Diagnosis:** Faecal impaction may be detected by an abdominal X-ray, or by a rectal or vaginal examination.
- **Treatment:** Faecal impaction must be treated by a health professional. The lower bowel has to be emptied and bowel transit time has to be speeded up as much as possible. A routine prevention programme should then be followed strictly.

The elderly, as we've seen, can have special problems with diet and activity; but following the advice given in the next chapter as much as possible will help you keep everything moving.

Chapter 5
Self-help Strategies

So far, we have looked at the bowel, at how it functions and some of the things that can go wrong, causing constipation. It's time now to look at all those things that go together to ensure healthy bowel function, to help you work out some self-help strategies to overcome the problem. Remember the five key elements to good bowel function? They are:

- THE COMMANDER – our brain, which controls all the body systems
- THE CONTENTS – the faeces
- THE CONDUIT – the bowel
- THE CONTAINER – the anorectum
- THE CONTROL – the muscle function

We need to look for strategies that will work on each of these key elements. These might include:

- The fibre in your food.
- The amount of fluids that you need to drink.
- Exercise and movement.

SELF-HELP STRATEGIES 45

- The best position for emptying your bowels.
- Getting your pelvic floor muscles into shape (more on this in Chapter 8).
- Making the right moves with your pelvic floor muscles (see Chapter 9).

FIBRE – FACTS AND FALLACIES

Those who suffer constipation generally eat less fruit and vegetables than other people. They also tend to drink less fluid overall, but drink more tea and coffee than others.

Constipated or not, most of us should increase our intake of dietary fibre by eating more fruits and vegetables and wholegrain products. Constipation may be prevented by eating a wide range of fibre-rich foods, rather than relying on a single source – such as wheat bran or dietary supplements.

If you are constipated, it's well worth the effort of taking a look at your diet and adjusting the fibre level, if necessary, by eating just such a wide range of fibre-rich foods. How can you tell if you are getting enough fibre in your diet? Look at your stool in the toilet bowl. If it floats, your fibre intake is OK. If it sinks, then you need to increase your dietary fibre.

READY! AIM! FIBRE!

What exactly is fibre? It's part of the cell structure within all plants. It is impossible for the body to digest fibre, so it acts like a sponge, absorbing water and swelling up. It has a direct effect on the function of the colon, producing a softer, bulkier stool – a floater, not a torpedo – as well as altering the speed at which it travels. Different foods contain different amounts and also different types of fibre . . . including cellulose, lignin, pectin, gums and others. A lot has been written about the effects of fibre on cholesterol and blood sugar levels, but we are only concerned here with how it affects good bowel function.

Simply adding unprocessed bran to your breakfast cereal is not going to solve your problem. It might form part of your programme to increase your fibre intake, but should not be the only thing that you do. This is especially so as you grow older.

NB: Elderly people should take care not to overload the colon by routinely sprinkling unprocessed bran over their food. This can literally be too much of a good thing. It may make things much worse by bulking out the stool too much, as well as absorbing some essential minerals from the body.

Raw wheat fibre (not too finely milled) is cheap and effective, but works best combined with an increase in fibre from a variety of sources. People who find bran unacceptable or inconvenient might prefer the other bulking agents mentioned in the box at the end of this chapter: 'Notions about potions and motions'.

HIGH FIBRE FOODS

Food	Serving	Fibre per g
Baked Beans	225g	16.4
Red Kidney Beans	50g raw weight	12.5
Butter Beans	50g raw weight	10.8
Chick Peas	50g raw weight	7.5
Peas	75g	9.0
Prunes	50g	8.1
Dried Figs	50g	9.3
Dried Apricots	50g	12.0
Blackberries	100g	7.3
Raspberries	100g	7.4
All Bran	40g	12.0
Lentils	50g raw weight	5.9
Baked Potato	200g	5.0
Sweet Corn	100g	5.7
Broccoli	100g	4.1
Dried Dates	50g	4.4
Passion Fruit	1 average	4.0
Wholemeal Bread	2 slices	5.1

48 LET'S GET THINGS MOVING

Wholemeal Pasta	50g raw weight	5.8
Bran Flakes	25g	4.3
Muesli	40g	4.4
Weetabix	40g	4.6
Runner Beans	100g	3.4
Brussels Sprouts	100g	2.9
Carrots	100g	3.1
Cabbage	100g	2.8
Apple	1 average	2.3
Banana	1 average	3.0
Pear	1 average	2.6
Orange	1 average	3.2
Brown Rice	50g	2.0
Porridge Oats	50g	3.4
Brown Bread	2 slices	3.9
Peanuts	25g	2.0
Brazil Nuts	25g	3.3

Use the table above to check the fibre content of the foods that you eat. Try to include high-fibre foods from several groups – vegetables, fruits, cereals and nuts. It's recommended that we eat 27–40g of fibre daily. To do this, you need to eat between 250–300g of fresh fruit and vegetables each day. If you choose to use a bulking agent – such as bran or Metamucil – start with a small dose. Remember, switching to a high-fibre diet is not quite as easy as switching brands of toothpaste. The change needs to be gradual to give your bowel a chance to adapt to the new and different stool that will be passing through.

You should also realise that there is nothing natural about taking all of your food fibre in one meal. It needs to be spread throughout the day.

HOW TO INCREASE YOUR FIBRE INTAKE

- Eat wholemeal or wholegrain bread in preference to white.
- Choose a breakfast cereal with high bran content.
- Fruit and vegetables are a <u>must</u> every day.
- Use pulses (beans, lentils, peas) more often; try them in casseroles, soups and salads.
- Choose brown rice instead of white.
- Potato skin has a lot of fibre; eat jacket potatoes and boil new potatoes in their skins.
- Do not overcook your vegetables; it can alter the form and the usefulness of their fibre.
- Fibre absorbs a lot of water – that's how it works – so increase your fluid intake to ensure there's enough to do the job; at least eight mugs or ten cups each day (see 'Fluid Facts' below).

HIGH-FIBRE ALTERNATIVES

If you really can't bring yourself to eat more high-fibre foods, you may prefer over-the-counter fibre supplements such as the Ispaghula group (which includes brands such as Fybogel and Metamucil) and Sterculia (which includes Normacol and has the same actions as the Ispaghula group). For more on such bulking agents and laxatives, see box at the end of this chapter.

NB: It is essential to increase fluid intake with all fibre supplements.

FLUID FACTS

Very few people drink the recommended amount of fluid – two litres each day. Some of us do not get enough exercise, so we rarely work up a thirst, regardless of what the beer advertisements on television would have us believe. We tend to drink from habit more than need – a set drink at breakfast, lunch and tea, with varying amounts in between.

Women who suffer from bladder control problems often cut down on their fluids to stop leaking or having to rush off to the toilet every ten minutes. This is not only bad for the bladder, but also bad for the bowel. If your constipation is due to slow transit time (see Chapter 6), this means that the stool spends more time than usual in the colon. Since the colon is the drying tank for the bowel, then it stands to reason that you are going to lose more water from the stool than other people.

The amount of water in your stool will be even less if you aren't drinking enough in the first place. It's a good idea to measure your daily intake for a few days, and keep a diary of the results to see whether you are drinking enough fluid. If not, it's time to up your intake of water and other fluids.

HOW TO INCREASE YOUR FLUID INTAKE

- Plan to increase fluids gradually.
- You don't have to drink huge glasses of water in a single go – keep a large covered glass on the sink and take a few sips each time you pass.
- Keep chilled water or mineral water in the fridge with a glass next to it.
- Cups tend only to hold about 200ml – try using mugs, which hold more, for hot drinks.
- Have a stock of your favourite drink on hand (but watch the calorie content).
- Alcohol should be avoided.
- Don't forget that many foods have a high fluid content, too – such as fruits like watermelons, grapes and oranges; soups, stews, jellies, custard and ice cream.
- Studies show that sufferers of constipation drink more caffeine beverages. Caffeine has a

52 LET'S GET THINGS MOVING

bad effect on many of the body systems, so it might be an idea to reduce your coffee, tea and cola intake to about four mugs a day in total.

MASSAGE

Mothers have been massaging the tummies of colicky babies forever. You don't have to be a baby to benefit; gentle massage over the abdominal area sometimes helps get things moving. Here's how to get started.

Lie with the upper half of your body supported by pillows. Place a pillow beneath your knees so that they are supported in a slightly bent position.

Your hands should be warm, and their pressure should be firm. You will probably be able to feel the bowel contents if you're constipated. Remember that the colon begins in the lower right-hand corner of the abdomen. This is where the massage should begin.

- Your abdomen should be bare. If you feel cold, cover yourself completely with a rug or blanket.
- Using a firm, gentle pressure, make large stroking movements up your right side, across the rib cage and down the left-hand side of the abdomen. This is the direction of movement along the colon. These large movements are called effleurage.
- These stroking movements can be followed

by small circular movements, always following the same direction as the bowel contents, Repeat each small circular movement about six times before changing your hand position.
- Continue the massage for about 10 minutes or until your hands get tired.

This massage should be a pleasant experience. If you feel any discomfort, stop immediately.

YOUR ACTIVITY LEVEL

Any period of inactivity – due to illness, for example, or a change to a more sedentary occupation – can cause constipation problems. This is because physical activity has a very definite and positive effect on peristalsis, particularly after eating. The gastro-colic reflex, which causes evacuation of the contents of the colon when food enters the stomach, is triggered not only by food or fluid entering the stomach, but also by activity. This is especially so when it follows a short period of inactivity, such as when we get up after being in bed overnight. This reflex sends a wave of peristalsis from the middle of the transverse colon down into the rectum.

SITTING PRETTY

Squatting – that's the best position to adopt in order to empty your bowels properly, and it's the one that is automatically used from early childhood in most developing nations. Toilets, as we know them, have only been used since the middle of the 1800s; and the fact that everybody in the UK has a pedestal model doesn't make them ideal. You might try to make an adaptor for your toilet, which will enable you to squat. Set foot supports about 15cm or six inches high, one on each side of the toilet, which could be made out of a variety of objects. When we squat on these supports, the pelvic floor is braced, providing support for the anus as it opens.

More on the part played by the pelvic floor, its muscles and how you can train them, in chapters 8 and 9.

Forearms help abdominal bracing

NOTIONS ABOUT POTIONS AND MOTIONS

Some foods act as laxatives, hurrying food and faeces through the bowel. These include prunes and prune juice, molasses, liquorice, chocolate, citrus, black coffee, alcohol and spices. You will know what works for you.

However, many people rely not on food but on commercial laxatives. An enormous amount of money is spent each year on laxatives in the Western world. Much of this laxative use is not necessary, and long-term use must be on the advice of your doctor.

Laxatives may be given orally in tablet or liquid form, or rectally by suppository or microenema. Laxatives are classified into different groups depending on how they work. These include:

- Simple bulking agents, eg: Ispaghula, Sterculia and Methykellulare.
- Faecal softeners, eg: Oral liquid paraffin.
- Osmotic agents, eg: Lactulase.
- Stimulants which act on the nerves and muscles of the bowel wall. These are often found in herbal or natural laxatives.

There may be a combination of these substances in oral and rectal laxatives.

Simple small doses of bulking agents are usually safe. These make stools 'teflon-coated' and easier to pass.

Much has been said about 'natural' products. Senna is a commonly used preparation found in herbal laxatives. It is refined from plants, and acts as a stimulant. Over a long period of continued use, it deposits a brown discolouration on the normal healthy bowel lining. In time, the bowel muscle relies on this stimulant to continue to squeeze the contents along. The fact that a product is 'natural' doesn't necessarily mean it is harmless and without any side effects, so you should consider carefully before taking herbal laxatives, particularly over the long term. Always check with your doctor or chemist and be sure that you read and understand the label before taking any medication.

Many people may require long-term combinations of laxatives to treat their symptoms of Slow Transit Constipation or Obstructed Defaecation (more on these problems in Chapters 6 and 7). This must be strictly under medical supervision. Suppositories are used to help poorly contracting rectums to empty properly. To be effective, the suppository must be inserted into the rectum, that is, past the anus. It must be placed next to the rectal wall, not in the faecal contents.

Chapter 6
'Slow Motion': Slow Transit Constipation

In Chapter 3, we took a very brief look at slow transit constipation (sometimes called colonic inertia). This is a problem affecting a minority of constipation sufferers, in which faeces move extra slowly through the colon, so slowly that fermentation takes place and extra gas is produced. This increases pressure within the bowel, and may cause abdominal pain and bloating.

This gas can slow things down even further, in a way that works a bit like the inner tube of a bicycle tyre. If you half fill the tube, the gas goes through; fully fill the tube and nothing can go through.

At times the bowel may be kinked like a garden hose. It may be stuck down in places by adhesions (bands of fibrous tissue sticking to organs which are caused by inflammation or injury). Such kinking and adhesions make it even more difficult for increased gas and faeces to move through the bowel. The longer contents remain in the colon, the more water is absorbed, and lumps of faeces may build up

SLOW TRANSIT CONSTIPATION
How problems develop

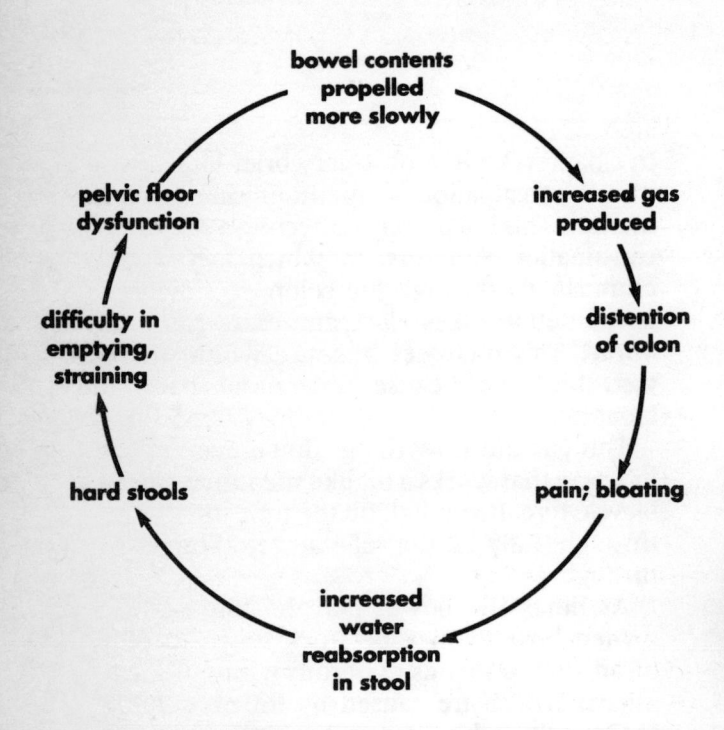

bowel contents propelled more slowly → increased gas produced → distention of colon → pain; bloating → increased water reabsorption in stool → hard stools → difficulty in emptying, straining → pelvic floor dysfunction → (bowel contents propelled more slowly) along the n-shaped colon, drying out and forming into hard 'pebbles' or 'boulders'. These are difficult to get rid of, and stools may only be passed once every three days or longer. Ninety per cent of the sufferers of this condition are women. The problem often starts in childhood or puberty, but can also begin later in life.

SYMPTOMS OF SLOW TRANSIT CONSTIPATION

These can include:

- Abdominal bloating, usually worse at the end of the day, requiring a two-size wardrobe.
- Pain caused by gas and faeces stretching the walls of the colon.
- Headache – this is very common.
- Gastric reflux (heartburn).
- Inability to finish a meal because of associated problems with the stomach.
- No urge to empty the bowels; or sometimes, even if the urge is present, little is actually passed.
- Bladder problems, particularly in passing urine.

Sometimes a bowel that has been overstretched over time becomes damaged, floppy, has weak muscle walls, and stretches more readily, causing even worse symptoms. This is called a **megacolon**. The passage of contents through a megacolon are slowed down – moving a little like a wide, slow river,

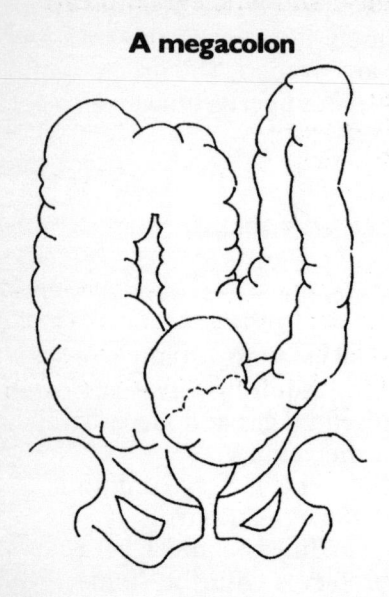

A megacolon

TREATMENT

This condition requires highly specialised investigation. Treatment includes dietary advice and prescribed medication to maintain bowel function and comfort, and simple measures will help up to 90 per cent of sufferers. Contrary to the usual advice, the intake of grain fibre should be reduced. Fibre in the form of fruit, vegetables, and salad vegetables is preferable to that of grain fibre, particularly

'SLOW MOTION' – SLOW TRANSIT CONSTIPATION 61

bran. Those foods that should be removed from the diet include:

- Wholemeal and wholegrain bread
- Muesli
- Bran
- Cabbage
- Brussels sprouts
- Broccoli stalks
- Dried fruit
- Nuts.

You'll feel better if you eat small amounts during the day rather than three standard meals. Surgery (see Chapter 11) may be required for those few who are not helped by these measures.

Chapter 7
Obstructed Defaecation

Is getting it out getting you down? Unlike Slow Transit Constipation, this is a constipation problem in which you want to go – but can't get it out. There are a number of possible reasons for this particular condition, which is called 'obstructed defaecation' and also tends to afflict women in particular. Such reasons may include the fact that:

- The body does not know faeces are there (no call of nature).
- The body does not know when to get rid of faeces, so that the rectum overfills.
- Or the body does not know how to expel faeces.

If you have a diseased rectum, or one that is far too large, then you will have great difficulty in emptying it. If the anorectum is damaged, or the muscles working to funnel and support the anal canal are damaged, you are not able to expel faeces. In many cases the problem is made worse because <u>both</u> these conditions may occur together.

OBSTRUCTED DEFAECATION 63

> ### INCONTINENCE
>
> Faecal incontinence – the inability to control one's bowel movements – may sound like the opposite problem to constipation. Oddly enough, however, it can be associated with obstructed defaecation, and sufferers may become incontinent of wind, mucus and faeces, in a way that can range from trivial to socially embarrassing to downright incapacitating. This can be a difficult problem to deal with. Treatment, which varies depending on the cause of the problem, may include medication, diet changes, specialised physiotherapy and, in selected cases, surgery.

Remember the symptoms of the problem may be that feeling that 'I want to go, but can't'; but may also include other bowel symptoms described earlier. Hold ups may occur because the blockage is happening at the final point of exit.

As well as severe difficulties in passing motions (using straining or hand pressure), you may pass small deformed stools, or have pressure feelings in the vagina. Sometimes bleeding and itchiness around the anus occur. It is not unusual to leak faeces or mucus on to your underwear. Pain is common, often of a nagging toothache kind; but may also be felt as a sharp rectal pain, or dragging pelvic pain.

There may be decreased vaginal sensation, an inability to retain tampons, and sex may be painful. You could also suffer from urinary symptoms (such as incontinence, frequency and urgency – see box 'Water, Water, Everywhere').

All of this could make you feel as though you're falling apart at the seams! This group of bowel symptoms is one of the most difficult to assess, and needs expert handling. Let's take a look at how these problems typically develop.

CAUSES

Obstructed defaecation may start in childbirth, with damage to the pelvic nerves and pelvic floor muscles. The overstretched pelvic floor moves down further than normal each time you attempt to go to the toilet. This pushes the anus and its support down beyond the proper limit. The end result, whenever you bear down in an attempt to defaecate, is a bit like trying to get toothpaste out of a tube by squeezing the wrong place, or when it's still got its lid on. This is called the Descending Perineum Syndrome.

A common form of obstructed defaecation is seen when the rectal lining and rectal wall closest to the vagina are thin and baggy. Passing a motion is difficult because the faeces move towards the vagina, and not down the anal funnel. This rectal pocket is called a **rectocoele**.

OBSTRUCTED DEFAECATION 65

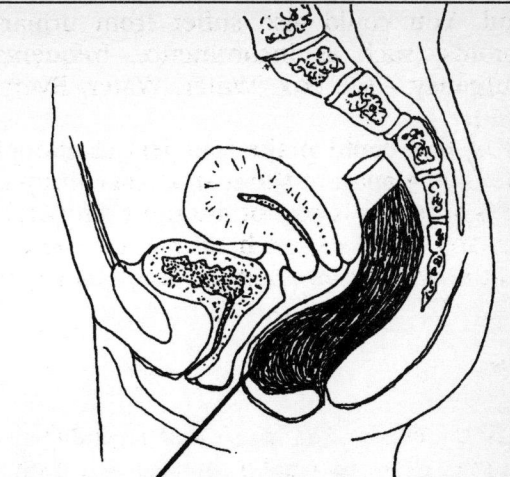

Forward pouching into the vagina – this is called a rectocoele

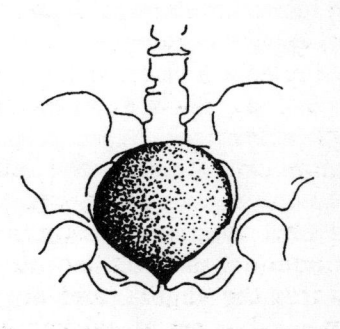

Large volume bladder

WATER, WATER, EVERYWHERE

There can be a relationship between certain bladder and bowel problems, which means that some bladder problems may improve dramatically when proper bowel function is restored. Many women, for example, have decreased bladder sensation, which means that excessive quantities of urine may accumulate in the bladder without its owner being aware of it. This can contribute to urinary frequency (having to 'go' often) and incontinence (inability to control the flow of urine). Such women (and men) often have megarectums, and have to strain to empty their bowels. Both these problems — large bladder volume and large rectal volume — often accompany Slow Transit Constipation or Obstructed Defaecation.

How can you tell if you have a large bladder volume? Measure the urine you pass first thing in the morning (simply squat on the floor and catch the urine in an ice cream container and measure with a measuring jug). Repeat this for two or three mornings to get an idea of your urine output. If it is greater than 500–600ml (about 1 pint), you have a large volume bladder, which could be putting quite a load on weak bladder walls and pelvic supports. Emptying it requires straining (abdominal pushing), putting extra pressure on the bladder and pelvic supports, and the whole cycle is repeated. 'Reverse' bladder training — remembering to

> empty your bladder four to six times a day — helps to prevent the bladder walls from becoming stretched, allowing the bladder to empty better. Specialised physiotherapy on the pelvic floor will help the bladder maintain its support and function. More about the pelvic floor in the next chapter.

The problem of obstructed defaecation can also arise simply because people do the wrong thing when they go to the toilet. To defaecate normally, we need to support and lift with our deep pelvic floor muscles, and relax the sphincters. Some people do quite the opposite, letting it all hang loose, or nearly the opposite, 'the uptight anus' (one which can't open properly).

Timing could also be causing the problem. You may have been putting off going to the toilet, ignoring the call of nature, perhaps for reasons of social embarrassment. But over time, if this behaviour continues, the normal emptying reflexes become weaker until the rectum finally does not respond to normal sensations or reflexes. The result: you can't go to the toilet.

A few rare people are born without nerve supply to some segments of the anorectum, which means that the normal emptying reflexes simply don't exist. This is called **Hirschsprung's Disease**.

DIAGNOSIS

People suffering from chronic defaecation difficulties or gut blockage (a backlog of faeces and gas) need medical treatment. To arrive at a diagnosis of your problem, your doctor may order functional bowel tests (to see how your bowel is working), such as anorectal physiology tests, proctoscopy or electrophysiological studies. More about these tests in Chapter 10.

OBSTRUCTED DEFAECATION

HOW OUTLET PROBLEMS DEVELOP

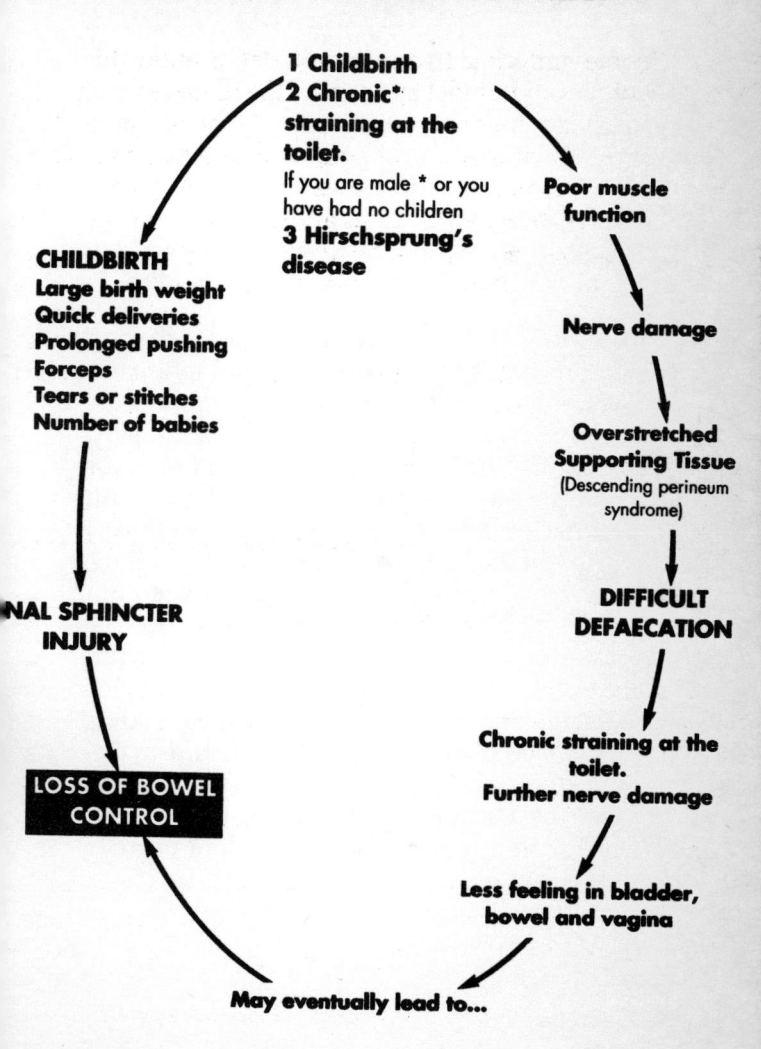

1. Childbirth
2. Chronic* straining at the toilet.

If you are male * or you have had no children

3. Hirschsprung's disease

↓

Poor muscle function

↓

Nerve damage

↓

Overstretched Supporting Tissue
(Descending perineum syndrome)

↓

DIFFICULT DEFAECATION

↓

Chronic straining at the toilet. Further nerve damage

↓

Less feeling in bladder, bowel and vagina

↓

May eventually lead to...

CHILDBIRTH
Large birth weight
Quick deliveries
Prolonged pushing
Forceps
Tears or stitches
Number of babies

↓

ANAL SPHINCTER INJURY

↓

LOSS OF BOWEL CONTROL

Chapter 8
The Part Played by Pelvic Floor Muscles

As we've seen, the pelvic floor muscles support the anorectal angle and hold the anal sphincters in the best possible position to empty the rectum, and they have other roles to play. They can be separated into lifting and opening and closing muscles. The lifting muscles support our pelvic organs as we exert ourselves during the day, for example walking, standing, lifting, sneezing, toileting. They also help to keep our rectum and bladder in the right place, so that we can pass urine and faeces efficiently, without straining. They also give support during childbirth, and are important in lovemaking. They may be damaged by childbirth and straining at stool, and can be weakened by spinal problems, a chronic cough or being overweight.

The greatest force on our pelvic floor muscles occurs during:

PELVIC FLOOR MUSCLES

1. Childbirth, when we bear down.
2. During defaecation, or when we strain.

} Emptying

3. During lifting, pushing and carrying heavy loads.
4. Sneezing, coughing.
5. Sporting activities, such as running and jumping.

} Effort

The key to good pelvic floor function is the part of the lifting muscle we call the deep supporting sling. It surrounds the urethra, vagina and anus. This muscle works or contracts when we get the feeling of lifting our vagina and anus. Some people work it by drawing up the sling, starting at the back and moving through to the front. You will learn how to do this in the section headed 'Can You Feel It Working?', overleaf. If you have a chronic cough, or are overweight, your muscles will need extra attention. If nerve damage has occurred, learning how to work this sling will help you slow down the deterioration that comes with bearing down, straining and ageing; improvement may be marked.

Like any group of muscles in the body, the pelvic floor muscles respond well to exercise programmes designed to improve function. These muscles must first be located and then be worked before you can learn to go to the toilet without straining.

PELVIC FLOOR MUSCLES AT WORK

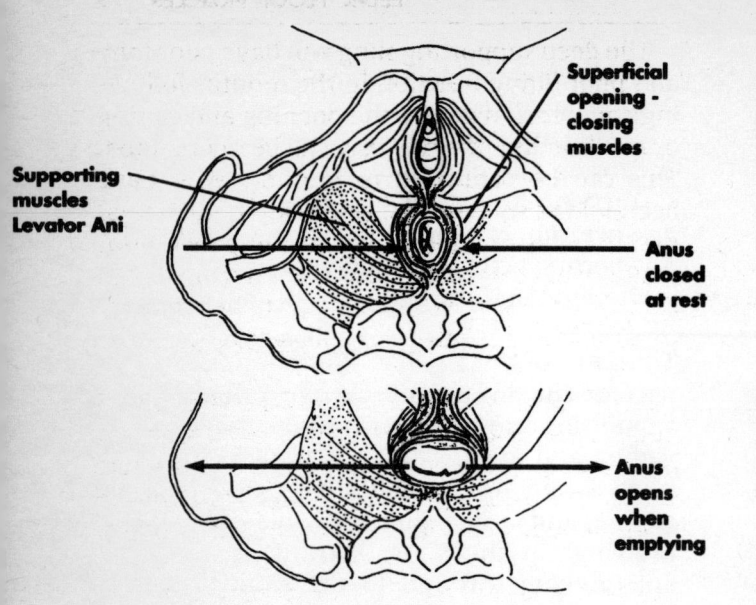

Superficial opening - closing muscles

Supporting muscles Levator Ani

Anus closed at rest

Anus opens when emptying

Levator Ani supports while anus opens

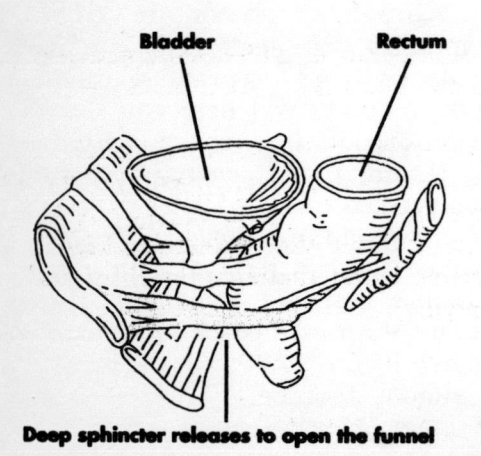

Bladder

Rectum

Deep sphincter releases to open the funnel

PELVIC FLOOR MUSCLES 73

The deep supporting sling will have poor tone and poor lifting function in the months following childbirth, whereas the opening and closing or quick action muscles may still be maintained. This can be confusing to mothers who have been told to squeeze their muscles in post-natal exercise classes. Good tone in the pelvic floor may mean that you get much better messages from your rectum when it needs to be emptied. In other words, the call of nature may be clearer.

The following programme will also teach you how to use the muscles around your waist to help brace your pelvic floor when you exert yourself or wish to defecate. Then you will be ready to learn two patterns of muscle activity:

1. Effort – when you lift, cough or sneeze.
2. Emptying – when you need to empty your bowel or give birth.

An easy way to organise your exercise programme is to think of the four Fs:

- Feel it working (muscle awareness)
- Find its exercise limit (maximise the sling support)
- Force this limit higher (learn to brace)
- Function better (patterns for effort and emptying).

74 LET'S GET THINGS MOVING

CAN YOU FEEL IT WORKING?

This can be quite a problem. When women are asked to squeeze up (contract) their pelvic floor muscles, one third of them actually bear down instead. This is not only the wrong action, it might be causing more and more pelvic weakness! So before you can build up the strength of your pelvic floor muscles you have to find out whether they are working as well as how. Here's how to do this:

Sit on the toilet with your knees wide apart. Start the flow of urine, then try to stop it. It should stop dead, not just slow down to a trickle.

Another way to find out whether these muscles are working is to look at them while trying to squeeze them up. You will need a mirror to do this. Propping yourself up on a bed in a half-sitting/half-lying pose is the best position for such an examination, as it involves less downward pressure on the pelvic floor than when you are standing or sitting on the toilet. Men will need to lift their penis and scrotum forward out of the line of vision.

Watch the whole perineum as well as the anus as you do a big squeeze and lift, and just see what happens. Everything should move in an upward direction, away from the mirror. The anus should pucker up like a purse-string being pulled tight.

If you don't seem to be able to see it working, try this. Pull up as though you were about to pass wind and the Queen has just walked into the room. Squeeze up to stop the wind from escaping and making a loud, embarrassing noise. Don't worry if you seem to be squeezing up the front passage as well as the back; it takes an enormous amount of muscle control to work one without the other, but you do hear some wondrous stories of what some people can do in this area! Now try to hold it for a few seconds. Men seem to have less trouble than women recognising that their pelvic floor muscles are working.

WOMEN ONLY

Women who leak urine while coughing or sneezing, usually have quite weak pelvic floor muscles. To feel such weak muscles contracting, it will almost certainly be necessary to use your fingers. Prop yourself up on the bed in the position described above. Use the index and middle fingers of your right or left hand, whichever suits you; make sure they are washed and clean, or use a disposable glove. Moisten the inserting fingers with saliva or a little lubricating jelly (not vaseline or face cream, as these can irritate the sensitive lining of the vagina). Gently slide your fingers into your vagina. Close your eyes and concentrate. Pull up your muscles as though you need to pass water and can't find a toilet. Can you feel any movement?

76 LET'S GET THINGS MOVING

If not, try the 'stopping your wind from making a loud noise in front of the Queen' routine, described above.

Still not sure whether it's working or not? Then try another trick. Imagine a long, sharp pin is being brought closer and closer to your anus. Try to squeeze up and pull yourself away from the pin as it comes closer and closer.

Still can't feel anything? Maybe your muscles have been overstretched by childbirth. Now gently push your fingers toward your back passage and try again to squeeze up. At the same time, try the 'stop your wind' exercise, and imagine that pin is about to prick your bottom. Don't remove your fingers just yet. While you are in a position to explore this area and its problems, just feel what happens when you cough. Feel all that downward pressure? You might even feel a bulging sensation. Gently bear down as though trying to use your bowels and feel the downward movement again. This is the exact opposite feeling to doing a pelvic floor contraction properly!

Now, immediately squeeze and lift up. You should feel a definite lifting movement, which should be upward and inward. You might be able to touch the tip of your cervix (it feels just like the tip of your nose); it sometimes moves upwards and away from your fingertips as you do a contraction.

If you still cannot feel a contraction, try placing the index finger of your other hand on to the tip of your tailbone at the back. Rest the thumb of the hand that is inside your vagina on your pubic bone and press it firmly down. Imagine that you are trying to pull these two points together. Do not hold your breath – this allows you to push down with your diaphragm. Continue breathing rhythmically in and out as you try to contract your pelvic floor muscles.

When you can finally feel those muscles contracting, no matter how tiny the movement seems to be, you are ready to begin your own, individually designed exercise programme.

FIND ITS LIMIT

Draw up the deep supporting sling muscles around the urethra, vagina and anus. Feel the lift and hold the lift for as long as you can (e.g. five to 10 seconds), then let go. When you're learning to lift you will only hold this contraction for a few seconds. These muscles need to be strengthened, and better still, need to build up staying power as you exert or empty. If you do not initially assess your muscle strength and endurance, you won't be able to progress your exercise programme. Having felt the muscle contract and lift, you now need to feel just how long you can hold the contraction/lift. Weak muscles must be given special attention and time to recover after each contraction. You should rest for 10 seconds or so between contractions.

FORCE IT HIGHER

No matter if you are able to lift the sling for five, 10, 20 or even 30 seconds or longer, only do a set of four repetitions at any one time. Increase the time you hold the lift so that your muscles relearn how to do this automatically. Do many sets during the day. You will need to use your fingers to assess and reassess your progress. Remember, your aim is not to build your squeeze pressure but to increase your endurance.

The increased tone and support you will gain should be sufficient to help your pelvic floor cope with bursts of heavy exertion such as defaecation, controlling a sneeze or lifting the groceries from shopping trolley to car boot.

In contrast, the opening and closing muscles can be squeezed and let go many more times in succession. They tighten quickly if it is impossible for you to pass wind discreetly, and they open when you are emptying. To work these muscles, you should tighten quickly, then let go. Do not tighten your buttocks. If you stand pigeon-toed with your knees together, it will be easier to feel the sphincter muscles and harder to use your buttock muscles.

WARNING

- Overdoing your exercises can cause muscle tiredness.
- Expect little progress around your period time – but don't give in.
- Whenever you are run down, so is your pelvic floor – don't expect miracles.
- Repeated coughing or sneezing (e.g. flu or hayfever) can set your programme back dramatically – don't be discouraged.

You have now learned the importance of the lifting muscles. If you have not felt any lift with your fingers you may need to see a physiotherapist who is specially trained in this area. She may suggest you use vaginal weights with 'feedback' strings designed to help you find your muscles by working in a particular way. With perseverance and time (often up to three months), the feeling of knowing what to do will come back.

As a bonus, working with the deep sling muscles will increase vaginal sensation during lovemaking. This is because it helps restore the function of a number of nerves and muscle-fibres damaged by childbirth, causing decreased sexual enjoyment.

HELPING THE PELVIC FLOOR MUSCLES

The pelvic floor muscles aren't the only ones you should be concerned with when defaecating. You can actually help support your pelvic floor with your side tummy muscles. This is called abdominal bracing and simply means, as it were, 'making your waist wide'. Weight lifters and others who lift heavy objects use this technique to support their back and pelvic floor. Pregnant women also rely on these muscles to increase abdominal pressure during defaecation, as well as bearing down in childbirth, as their tummy muscles are too stretched to contract.

The link between our lip muscles and sphincter (opening and closing muscles) is an interesting one, because we unconsciously copy what our sphincters are doing by pursing or opening our lips. We must pull up our pelvic floor when we want to lift, so we keep our lips closed. When emptying our bowels and giving birth, we keep our lips slightly open. This is the way women should bear down when they are in labour, being aware of the differing actions of the lifting and opening and closing muscles (see 'Brace, Open Out, Grunt' overleaf).

FUNCTIONING BETTER

As we've seen, the strain on the pelvic floor muscles is greatest during childbirth, defaecation and straining (emptying); and when lifting, pushing, carrying heavy loads, sneezing, coughing and jumping (effort).

Let's look at how we can help our pelvic floor during these activities and maximise support during the effort pattern, when the load on it is greatest – when lifting, carrying or pushing:

When you lift:

1. Keep your mouth closed
2. Brace your abdominal muscles
3. Pull up your pelvic floor
4. Exhale on completion of task

} all at once

Some women even learn to sneeze like this, with their lips closed, so they do not lose support and let urine escape and wet their pants. If you get lazy and forget your patterns, your function will deteriorate. If you strain, with time you may lose urine or wet your pants; have rectal pain and may even soil.

Now we will look at the second of our patterns – the emptying pattern – and this will follow when we understand good defaecation dynamics, explained in the following chapter.

Chapter 9
Good Defaecation Dynamics

Most children know how to use their tummy and pelvic floor muscles instinctively. Some of us forget the knack, and have to relearn it. Here's a run-down on how to do what should come naturally. When things are working properly, we should become pear-shaped when we defaecate (that is, the muscles widen and thicken in our lower body, making us look broader). Do you? Here's how to tell.

- Sit forward on a chair.
- Place one hand on your waist, resting on the hip bone.
- Place your other hand over the lower abdominal wall (just above the pubic bone).

Now pretend you are going to the toilet, bracing and using the muscles you would normally use. Feel what happens under both hands. You should feel a widening of your waist. At the same time, your abdominal wall should push forward under your other hand, as you make your anal muscles open. You are feeling your

GOOD DEFAECATION DYNAMICS 83

anterior abdominal muscles relax (and bulge) as you open. When we actually do defaecate, we should perform these actions unconsciously, with only a moderate abdominal effort.

But as we've said, it's easy to lose this basic pattern over time, particularly if we have poor organ and muscle support and decreased sensation in these areas. The result: we have to strain to use our bowels. We may not always be aware we're doing it.

Use the following checklist to see if you are straining to use your bowels. When you defaecate:

- Are you gulping in a breath of air and keeping lips closed tight?
- Are you sucking in your stomach muscles and supporting them with your hands?

If so, then you are actually making it harder for yourself to defaecate, not easier. You are pulling up and closing off the anus. This means your abdominal muscles have to work harder to push faeces through, with little success.

PUTTING IT ALL TOGETHER

Here's how to relearn the right way to empty your bowels.

1. Sit on a chair with both hands over the front of your stomach.

2. Draw up the sling (pelvic floor muscles).
3. Relax the sling, noting what happens to the abdominal wall. It should bulge.
4. Keeping your hands in place, imagine you are opening your anal muscles – **make the anus wide**. You should feel a greater swelling/tension/bulge underneath your hands as you do this.
5. Now move one hand to your waist. This time, when you open your anal muscles, feel the bulge under your front hand and the widening as you widen your waist. This is the normal pattern – you should resemble a pear. This is what should happen when you go to the toilet successfully. It is known as **brace and open out**.
6. Keep your lips slightly open and your teeth apart. This will help your anal muscles relax and release faeces. A relaxed jaw means an open pelvic floor. Breathe out. (So **brace and open out** is followed by **grunt!**)
7. Pull up the anorectal muscles as you finish emptying. This will improve the closing reflex and **turn off the switch**.
8. Remember those three simple instructions – **brace, open out, grunt!**

If you have symptoms of obstructed defaecation or are simply having trouble 'getting it out', you may need to work a little harder.

GOOD DEFAECATION DYNAMICS 85

THROAT CLOSED

FOREARM SUPPORT

DIAPHRAGM MOVES DOWN

ABDOMINAL BRACING/BULGING

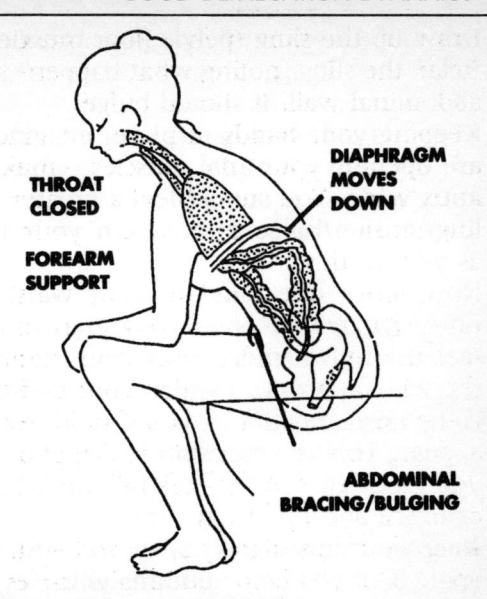

LEARNING HOW TO 'PUMP-BRACE'

These abdominal bracing muscles are very important in normal defaecation. They are very weak in people who chronically strain, whose muscle awareness is lessened.

If you draw in your stomach muscles without bracing, you will find it harder to open your anus (this may occur in the 'uptight anus' problem!). Learn to brace quickly; learn to hold the brace for some time (10–20 seconds).

If the normal emptying pattern has been lost and you're straining, you must learn to regain it. Here's how:

86 LET'S GET THINGS MOVING

1. To move the faeces into the rectal funnel, quick-acting bracing and opening is useful. This is called **pump/brace**. Do not consciously hold your breath; your diaphragm will move down at this time.
2. Brace and open out three or four times in succession. This can only work when the faeces are in the rectum and are ready to come out.
3. Sustain your bracing and opening out while you feel the contents going through the anus.
4. You may not think you are finished when you really are. Check this by bracing and opening several times; this will evacuate the stool if present. Do not strain, however strong the desire. If nothing comes away, what you are feeling may well be prolapsed lining of the rectum. Straining will make this worse, and further weaken your support.
5. To end the emptying and 'turn off the switch', draw up firmly with your supporting muscles.

Through body awareness, understanding and practice, this function will improve. However, you may well need specialised help from a physiotherapist.

HOW TO EMPTY A MEGARECTUM

If you have a megarectum, common problems, as we've seen, can include:

GOOD DEFAECATION DYNAMICS

- Delayed feeling of rectal contents.
- Loss of normal reflexes, so that soiling occurs; or
- Diarrhoea resulting from mucus and liquid faeces passing round a hard stool in the rectum.

Both conditions may need to be treated by oral laxatives, suppositories or enemas so that the rectum may be kept empty, and not enlarge further (this is important because such enlarging can lead to an overstretched rectum which doesn't give its owner any warning that it needs to be emptied).

You also have to learn to defaecate without straining. This may include:

1. Emptying 'on spec' at intervals during the day, using 'bracing and opening' (pump/brace).
2. Effective emptying using pump/brace with or without medication (rectal laxatives).
3. Sometimes by 'milking the contents', i.e., alternating **pump-brace/open** with **draw up/close**, you may still be able to feel even more faeces in the rectum. Indeed, wiping your anus after toileting often brings on another wave of movement and further contents are passed. These two methods increase pelvic floor sensitivity, so that you will be better able to 'feel' faeces in the rectum.

88 LET'S GET THINGS MOVING

LEARNING THE PATTERN

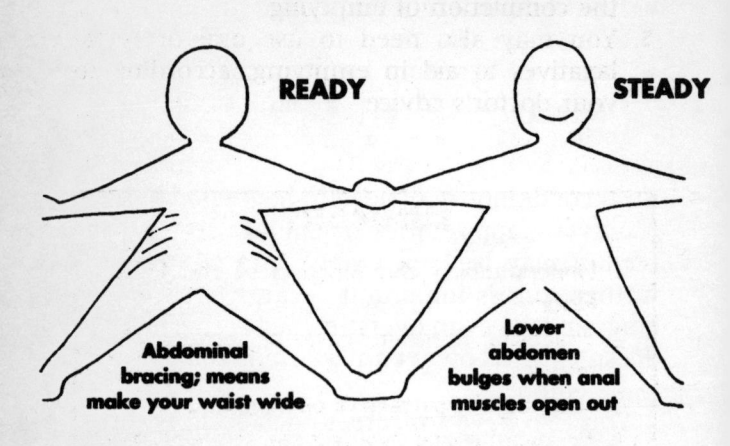

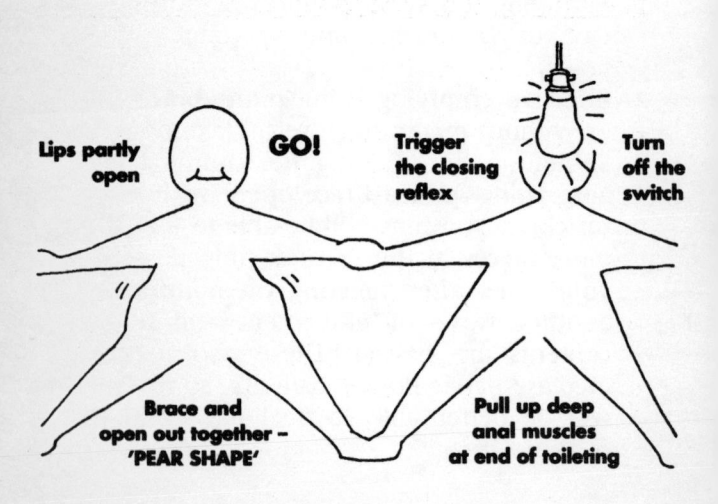

READY **STEADY**

Abdominal bracing; means make your waist wide

Lower abdomen bulges when anal muscles open out

Lips partly open **GO!** **Trigger the closing reflex** **Turn off the switch**

Brace and open out together – 'PEAR SHAPE'

Pull up deep anal muscles at end of toileting

4. Don't forget to increase the closing reflex by drawing up the muscles and rectal lining at the completion of emptying.
5. You may also need to use oral or rectal laxatives to aid in emptying, according to your doctor's advice.

SUMMARY

1. Understanding the function of the Pelvic Floor.
2. Practising Position Sense, or locating the muscles.
3. Learning the pattern of opening out.
4. Recognising and avoiding the straining pattern.
5. Understanding the **pump/brace** concept.

Chapter 10
Tests: Searching for Clues

In recent years various medical tests have been developed or adapted to help diagnose the causes of constipation and to show how well the bowel is functioning. Many patients will not need these tests, which are usually ordered only if the problem cannot be solved by simple means. But, just in case you ever need to know, here's a quick guide to such tests.

X-RAY TESTS

These tests are used to detect any blockages and assess the state of the bowel and any damage to it. In some cases, the specialist may order them if he thinks there may be a history of bowel cancer or polyps (growths on the colon and rectum).

There are two types of these tests:

1. **Simple X-ray** of the abdomen.
2. **Barium Enema** (Air Contrast).

This latter test is undertaken in an X-ray department, and takes about an hour. It gives a good, clear picture of the overall structure of your colon, but cannot always be relied upon to show problems of the lining of the bowel, e.g. polyps. You have to prepare carefully with diet and medication before undergoing a barium enema, to ensure the large bowel is empty. Barium and air are introduced into the rectum, which can be uncomfortable. Your body position will be altered several times during this hour, so that every part of the colon and rectum can be seen. Afterwards you will be instructed to empty your bowel. You may find it takes several days before all the light grey test material passes through.

ENDOSCOPY

These are tests which involve the insertion of thin, flexible tubes through which light can travel, allowing the specialist to see inside the body without invasive major surgery. Two types are used to diagnose bowel problems:

1. **Sigmoidoscopy.** This lets the specialist look at the rectum using a special tube that is inserted through the anus. It is not pleasant, but is important in excluding problems in the anorectum. In experienced hands, it helps assess the instability of the rectum or its lining, which can play a part in constipation.

2. **Colonoscopy.** This is the test the specialist uses when he wants to see the lining of the bowel from the anus to where the small and large bowel join. It gives a very accurate view of diseases affecting this lining (such as polyps), and allows the specialist to see any overall changes in the size and length of the bowel, e.g. megacolon. This test uses a flexible tube with a special camera attached which can follow the coils of the colon, allowing every nook and cranny to be seen. Some form of anaesthetic is always used in this procedure, which takes between 10 minutes and one hour. It is usually carried out in a day hospital. It is essential to follow your doctor's instructions on diet and medication prior to the procedure.

FUNCTIONAL TESTS

These are tests which your doctor may order to see how well your bowels are working or functioning. They include:

1. **Colon Transit Time.** If you have had problems for a long time, your doctor may order a Colon Transit Time test. This is a very important test which can show whether you have a slow bowel generally, or if you have an outlet problem (obstructed defaecation), or whether you indeed have a bowel problem at all. You will be asked to swallow

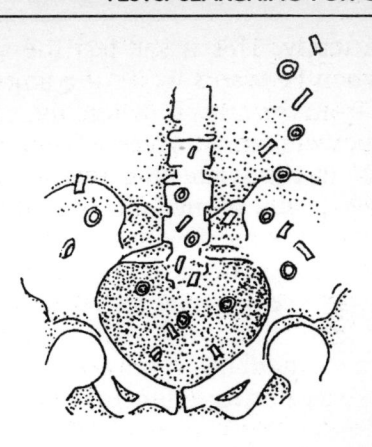

Radio opaque shapes used to determine colon transit time

radio opaque markers, and one or more plain X-rays are taken; these markers show up under X-ray and plot the path of faeces through the colon. This test must not be performed if there is any chance of your being pregnant.

2. **Anorectal Physiology.** This test investigates anorectal tone, elasticity, sensation and reflexes. It is indicated if constipation commenced in childhood. By using a small pressure-sensitive rectal tube, the anal muscles are tested at rest and when contracting. The sensation and capacity of the lower part of the rectum may also be tested, along with the involuntary anal muscle reflexes. Sometimes, the nerve endings to the anorectal muscles are absent, which means that the

lower bowel cannot empty. This is a rare condition called **Hirschsprung's Disease** (see Chapter 7), which is diagnosed by a biopsy of the rectal muscle.

3. **Electrophysiological Studies.** These are electrical tests of nerves and muscles in the pelvic region which can only be done by very experienced people. They can be painful as needles may be used. These tests show nerve or muscle damage commonly related to childbirth, and are useful in the case of faecal incontinence.

SOLVING THE PUZZLE

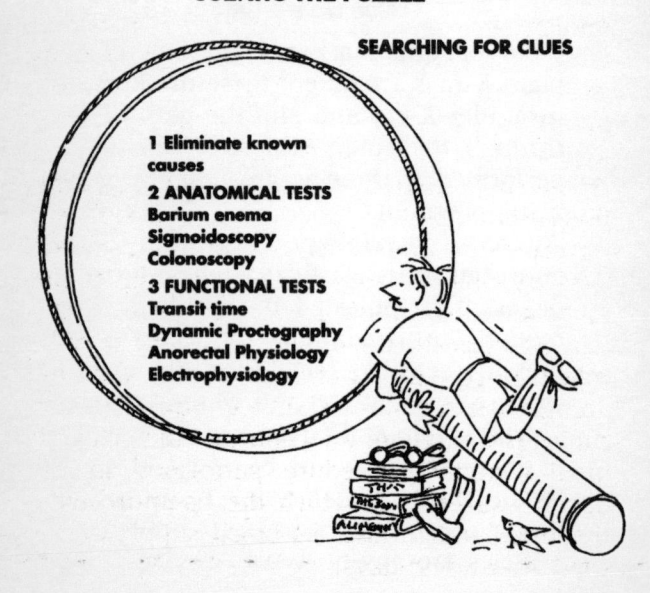

SEARCHING FOR CLUES

1 Eliminate known causes

2 ANATOMICAL TESTS
Barium enema
Sigmoidoscopy
Colonoscopy

3 FUNCTIONAL TESTS
Transit time
Dynamic Proctography
Anorectal Physiology
Electrophysiology

Chapter II
When Surgery is Needed

Surgery is considered only after the problem has been thoroughly and expertly assessed. The majority of people with defaecatory difficulties can be helped by non-surgical means, such as those outlined in this book. If, however, your doctor thinks that an operation is necessary to treat your problem, be sure that you understand exactly what is being proposed. Ask him to explain the procedure with diagrams, so you can see what is to be done and how it will help you.

This chapter is intended to explain the operations used in the treatment of constipation. Let's start from the anus and work up to the colon.

Many anal problems contribute to difficulties in defaecation, causing anal or perineal pain and unsatisfactory emptying. Surgery may be called for to treat fissures or tears in the anal lining; to drain abscesses; to control haemorrhoids (by excision, injection or 'rubber banding', a minor procedure performed in the doctor's surgery, in which the haemorrhoidal tissue is banded, loses its blood supply and is shed after a few days).

Prolapsed rectal lining, which may be blocking or plugging the anus, may also be rubber banded, allowing the faeces an unimpeded passage out of the body after this prolapsed lining is shed.

Sometimes the involuntary anal muscle is just too tight to function properly, and a small cut helps the opening and closing muscles do their job efficiently. This is called a **sphincterotomy**.

If you remember, a common form of obstructed defaecation occurs when the rectal lining and rectal wall closest to the vagina are thin and baggy, forming a 'pocket' called a rectocoele. In such cases, the rectal wall may be surgically repaired from the vagina or from the anorectum.

- **Rectopexy:** When the whole rectal wall hangs down and causes a holdup in proceedings it may be surgically repaired through an abdominal incision or through the rectum. The rectum may be drawn up and secured to the lower spine to help prevent its downward passage during defaecation. This is called a rectopexy and is used *only* in selected cases.
- **Proctectomy:** This operation may be performed on megarectums which cannot empty. In such cases, the rectum may be removed, and the colon then attached to the anus. This soon becomes a 'new' rectum.
- **Colectomy:** This procedure is performed to relieve severe symptoms associated with

slow transit constipation which are unable to be controlled medically. Here the colon is removed and the small bowel is attached to the rectum, allowing contents to be easily passed four to six times a day. However, if the rectum is very damaged and can no longer squeeze the faeces out, then a new rectum may be made from the small bowel. This is called a pouch.

- **Colostomy** is the term used when the colon is diverted out onto the skin surface. A bag is placed over the opening to collect faeces. It is used when the anorectum is too damaged or diseased to be repaired. It is *not* generally used in the surgical treatment of constipation.
- **Ileostomy** refers to the diversion of the small bowel to the outside of the body. A bag is also used to collect the contents of the small bowel, which are in liquid form. It is used when the colon and anorectum are in such poor condition they can no longer move contents along effectively. It may be considered only when symptoms are very severe.

PHYSIOTHERAPY MANAGEMENT

Surgery, as we've seen, is by no means your first or only option with defaecation difficulties. Physiotherapy can play a vital part. Specially trained physiotherapists may be able to help you to maximise your pelvic floor support when there is a problem with prolapse or poor bladder and bowel function. There are treatment methods to help reduce pain associated with poor pelvic floor support, and to re-educate muscles in the function of defaecation. Physiotherapy is useful before and after pelvic organ surgery; this treatment may include the use of vaginal weights, muscles stimulation and biofeedback. Specialised treatment methods are presently being researched, and their availability will increase over the next few years.

Glossary

Adhesions: Webs or bands of fibrous tissues which stick to organs, caused by inflammation or trauma.

Alimentary Tract: Digestive tube from the mouth to the anus.

Anal Sphincter: Opening and closing muscles of the anus, both involuntary and voluntary muscles.

Anismus: Failure of the anal sphincters to open, and to expel faeces.

Anorectum: The last 5 inches (12cm) of bowel where faeces are stored, and approx. 1–2 inches (2–5cm) of canal, which contents move through, before being expelled.

Anus: The outlet of the rectum lying in the fold between the buttocks, approximately 2 inches (5cm) long.

Banding: Rubber bands placed on haemorrhoidal or prolapsed rectal lining to 'unplug' the anus, by causing the banded portion to shrivel and be shed.

Biopsy: Removal of a piece of living tissue for microscopic examination.

Bladder: The hollow muscular organ where urine is stored.

Caecum: The first part of the large bowel which accepts liquid contents from the ileum.

Chyme: Partly digested food and chemicals in liquid, found in the stomach and small bowel.

Colectomy: The surgical removal of all or part of the large bowel.

Colon: The large bowel from ileum to rectum, approximately 60 inches (1.5 metres) long.

Colon Transit Time: The time taken for digested food to pass from the caecum to rectum.

Colonic Inertia: A much slower than normal large bowel.

Colostomy: An opening on the skin surface over which a bag is placed, allowing semi-solid bowel contents to pass from the colon to the exterior.

Descending Perineum Syndrome: The lack of pelvic support resulting from nerve damage. Defaecation becomes very difficult and there may be associated urinary problems.

Diverticular Disease: These are pockets in the wall of the large bowel which may become inflamed and infected with stagnant faeces.

Episiotomy: The surgical cutting of perineal tissue between the vagina and anus during childbirth.

Faeces: Formed waste products from the bowel.

Flatulence: Excessive gas in the intestines.

Faecal Impaction: Dry, hard lumps of faeces collecting in the rectum, making it very

GLOSSARY

difficult for the anorectum to expel.

Gastrocolic Reflex: Movement of contents from the colon into the rectum when food enters the stomach, usually most obvious at breakfast.

Haemorrhoids: Engorged veins resting on anal cushions (supports), or higher in the lining of the anorectum.

Hirschsprung's Disease: An area of anorectum without the normal nerve supply, so normal function is not possible.

Hormones: These are chemical substances secreted by the body, and may be involved in digestion or in directing sexual development and function.

Hysterectomy: The surgical removal of the uterus.

Ileostomy: An opening over which a bag is placed to collect liquid contents from the small bowel, used when the colon and anorectum are diseased beyond repair.

Ileum: The last part of the small bowel, from 15ft (4.5m) to 31ft (9m) long.

Incontinence: Involuntary loss of urine or faeces or both.

Irritable Bowel Syndrome: This occurs when the normal orderly movement of contents through the large bowel is frequently disturbed.

Jejunum: The part of the small bowel between the duodenum (near the stomach) and the ileum (near the large bowel); about 8ft (2.4m) long.

Laxatives: These are different groups of drugs to help relieve and treat constipation.

Levators: These are broad, thin muscles that help to form and support the floor of the pelvis.

Megacolon: A colon that is much wider and often longer than the normal colon.

Megarectum: A large, wide, thin-walled rectum.

Motility: This is the movement of food and chemicals through the alimentary tract.

Obstructed Defaecation: Difficulty in expelling faeces from the anorectum.

Oesophagus: The muscular tube from the mouth to the stomach, approximately 9 inches (23cm) long.

Pelvic Floor Muscle: The complex group of supporting, and opening and closing muscles, involved in urinary, sexual and anorectal function.

Perineum: This is the superficial tissue from the vulva to anus in the female, and from the scrotum to anus in the male.

Peristalsis: Contraction of the muscular walls in the alimentary tract necessary to push food and gases along.

Polyps: Benign, pre-malignant or malignant growths commonly found in the colon and rectum.

Pyloric Sphincter: This is a muscular ring allowing contents to pass from the stomach to the duodenum.

Rectal Instability: This occurs when the rectal

muscle and lining prolapse and lose support, making defaecation difficult and painful.

Rectocoele: This is a poorly supported rectal wall, which 'pockets' faeces, and pushes forward into the vagina.

Rectopexy: A surgical procedure used to attach a prolapsed rectum firmly to the sacrum or backbone.

Sigmoid Colon: An S-shaped part of the descending colon leading to the rectum. It can act as a 'brake' on the movement of faeces to the rectum.

Slow Transit Constipation: see Colonic Inertia.

Sphincterotomy: A surgical procedure used to release a tight internal or involuntary anal sphincter.

Stool: Another term for faeces.

Suppository: A rectal medication shaped like a pellet. It is inserted into the rectum to help it empty.

Urethra: This is the opening from the bladder, allowing urine to pass to the exterior.

Uterus: Womb.

Vagina: This is the genital opening leading from the uterus to the exterior.

ROBINSON FAMILY HEALTH

All your health questions answered in a way you really understand.

Titles available from booksellers or direct from Robinson include:

Arthritis: What *Really* Works
Dava Sobel & Arthur C. Klein
1–85487–290–7   £7.99

Asthma
Megan Gressor
1–85487–386–5   £2.99

Bad Backs: A Self-Help Guide
Leila Henderson
1–85487–388–1   £2.99

Bulimia Nervosa: A Guide to Recovery
Dr Peter Cooper
1–85487–171–4   £5.99

Headaches: Relief at Last
Megan Gressor
1–85487–391–1   £2.99

Let's Get Things Moving: Overcoming Constipation
Pauline Chiarelli and Sue Markwell
1–85487–389–X   £2.99

Massage for Common Ailments
Penny Rich
Illustrated in full colour
1–85487–315–6   £4.99

Menopause Made Easy
Kendra Sundquist
1–85487–383–0   £2.99

Pregnancy and Birth
Kerrie Lee
1–85487–390–3　　　　　£2.99

Overcoming IBS
Dr Christine P. Dancey & Susan Backhouse
1–85487–175–7　　　　　£5.99

Practical Aromatherapy
Penny Rich
Illustrated in full colour
1–85487–315–6　　　　　£4.99

The Recovery Book: A Self-Help Guide for Recovering Alcoholics, Addicts and Their Families
Al J. Mooney, Arlene Eisenberg & Howard Eisenberg
1–85487–292–3　　　　　£9.99

Women's Waterworks
Pauline Chiarelli
1–85487–382–2　　　　　£2.99

You *Can* Beat Period Pain
Liz Kelly
1–85487–381–4　　　　　£2.99

How to Order

To order a book, please send a cheque (made out to Robinson Publishing Ltd) or postal order to the address below, adding 50p per title for postage and packing. Send to: **Family Health, Robinson Publishing Ltd, 7 Kensington Church Court, London W8 4SP.**

While this information was correct at the time of going to press, details may change without notice.